Portfolio Assessment and Evaluation

Developing and Using Portfolios in the K–6 Classroom

Written by Janine Batzle
Edited by Barbara Maio
Illustrated by Terri Rae

Table of Contents

Part I Why Use Portfolios?

1. Introduction 4

2. A Change of Perspective 8

3. The Basic Principles of Assessment and Evaluation 12

Part II Working With Portfolios

4. Portfolio Essentials 22
   What Is a Portfolio?
   Types of Portfolios
   When Does a Teacher Find Time for Portfolios?
   How Are Portfolios Developed?
   Where Are Portfolios Developed?
   Who Is Involved in Portfolios?
   The Student's Role in Portfolio Development

5. Ways to Assess and Evaluate 34
   Building Portfolios

6. What to Do With Portfolios 58
   Organizing Portfolios
   Passing on Portfolios
   Portfolios and Report Cards
   Reporting to Parents

Part III Portfolios in Context

7. Portfolio Assessment and a Balanced Literacy Program 64
   A Balanced Literacy Program
   Experiences That Promote Literacy Development

8. The Development of Writing, Spelling and Reading 74
   The Three Stages of Writing Development
   Spelling as a Part of Writing
   The Reading Process
   The Three Stages of Reading Development

Part IV Resources

9. Forms and Checklists 98

10. Bibliography 122

CTP ©1992, Creative Teaching Press, Inc., Cypress, CA 90630

Part I
Why Use Portfolios?

1. Introduction

*Portfolio assessment and evaluation celebrates and documents what the child **can** do!*

Portfolio assessment is the most positive, dynamic form of evaluation used in education today. This method of evaluation celebrates and documents what the child *can* do. The teacher and the child become a collaborative team in the evaluation process. Together they explore, document, and reflect on the progress of the child. The child's ownership of the process is highly valued. Teacher judgment is a significant means of evaluating a child's learning.

The purpose of this book is to present the basic principles and methods of portfolio assessment and evaluation. A classroom conducive to portfolio development is described, and information is discussed which empowers the teacher to be an effective evaluator.

This book is intended to be an open-ended resource and a guide to help a teacher in the process of implementing portfolios in the classroom.

Becoming Empowered

Moving into portfolio assessment and evaluation takes time! Teachers need to work through this change at a comfortable pace. It involves forming a classroom which promotes a balanced literacy program (chapter 7), and where assessment and evaluation are a necessary part of the day-to-day functioning.

Portfolios flourish in a classroom where the teacher understands how children learn and develop and is knowledgeable about authentic methods of evaluating their progress.

Moving into portfolio asessment and evaluation takes time!

These portfolios will be more than work folders filled with student samples. They will guide instruction and give insight into a child's decision-making.

In addition, teachers need the freedom to take risks, make mistakes, and reflect on what they are experiencing. Administrators are the key. They can help teachers make this change by trusting teachers and providing a safe environment in which to develop professionally.

Laying the Foundation

As a teacher or a school endeavors to move into portfolio assessment and evaluation, it is important to discuss and explore the following:

1. **Define your belief system.** A look at philosophy is an important first step. What do you believe the school experience should be? What is the role of the teacher? How do children learn? How does language and all of its processes develop? What are the indicators of a good reader and writer?

2. **Know the community.** Know the children you work with. Talk to their parents, spend time in their community, and visit their homes. In order to be effective, all goals, instruction, and evaluation must be developed with the students in mind.

3. **Determine goals for your situation.** These goals should reflect your philosophy and the needs of the children at your school. Teachers and administrators take a collaborative responsibility to define these goals. You should see the school philosophy *in action* in the classroom.

4. **Align assessment and evaluation with instruction, goals and philosophy.** When this happens assessment and evaluation become tools for guiding instruction and sharpening, changing or modifying a school's philosophy and goals.

Our Beliefs
Our Community
Our Goals

As evaluation measures indicate a need for change, goals and instruction are redefined. The diagram below shows this cycle.

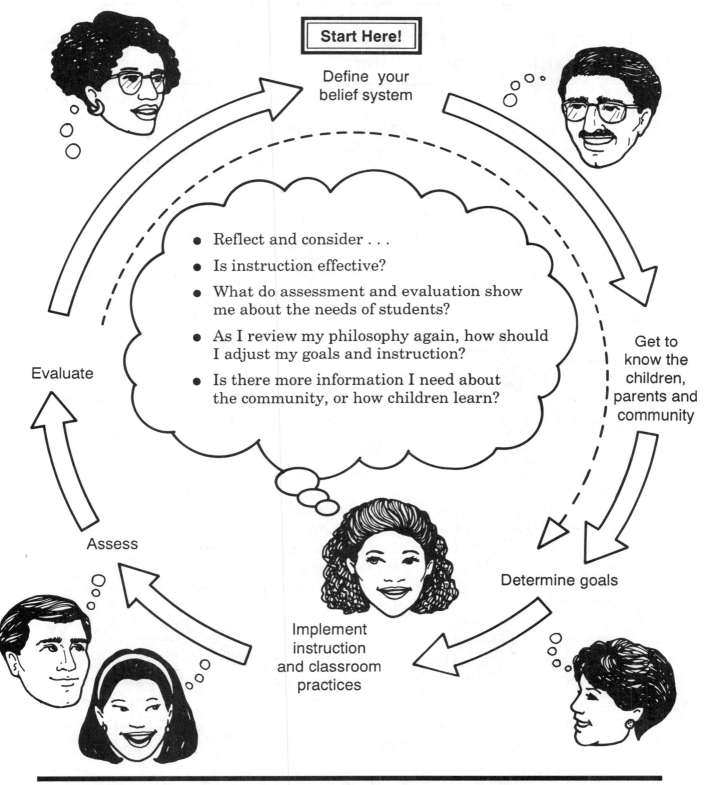

Start Here!

Define your belief system

Get to know the children, parents and community

Determine goals

Implement instruction and classroom practices

Assess

Evaluate

- Reflect and consider . . .
- Is instruction effective?
- What do assessment and evaluation show me about the needs of students?
- As I review my philosophy again, how should I adjust my goals and instruction?
- Is there more information I need about the community, or how children learn?

2. A Change of Perspective

Education's Past History With Assessment and Evaluation

A Classroom Snapshot

The classroom is absolutely silent. There are frowns on little faces, fingers twisting strands of hair over and over, teeth gnawing at bottom lips, wiggling bodies, and the steady rhythmic motion of knees moving up and down. The classroom looks unusual. Desks, previously placed in centers and clusters, are arranged in rows. Each child huddles over a test booklet, tightly grasping a yellow #2 pencil. The teacher walks among her first graders encouraging completion of the test.

Rey looks particularly puzzled. He raises his hand, "Ms. B., there is something wrong with my test book!"

"What's the matter with your book, Rey?"

He looks up with big, wide eyes. "It doesn't have pictures with the words! There's supposed to be pictures!"

By this time the entire class is listening and identifying with his observation. Ms. Batzle looks down at the child, "What a thinker you are to figure that out, but go ahead and give it a try anyway."

Rey persists, "We always read with pictures."

Ms. Batzle thinks back over the school year's experiences and the learning that has taken place. How many times, when she listened to the children read, had she reminded them to look at the pictures and to make their best guess? Now the children are faced with a standardized test with no match between the test, instruction, and the materials used in the classroom. Her class was used to talking, listening, and even singing as they worked during the school day. Normally, the room arrangement encouraged collaboration and many hands-on experiences. Anecdotal records and samples collected in the classroom showed Rey's literacy development and his growing appetite for reading and writing. How could this test possibly measure Rey's growth? What was its purpose? What did it really tell about Rey and his growing competence as a reader?

The standardized test is limited—incapable of measuring Rey's true abilities. The test presents a "moment in time" view of what Rey *couldn't* do with little evidence of what he could do.

The Teacher and the Student, Not the Test!

The educational system has allowed measures outside the classroom to determine the growth and progress of students. These measures are used to assure the public of the school's accountability. Tests, however, can only show the growth of a student at a given "moment in time." When educators use this limited measure to make overall judgments concerning achievement, progress is defined within a very narrow view.

In a school system, teachers are the most qualified participants to know the whole child and observe progress over time. Students are the most qualified to understand the inner reasons for their responses. Tests can be a part of evaluation, but they should only support, not define, the teacher's judgment (Anthony, et al., 1991). **The primary responsibility of assessment and evaluation belongs to the teacher and the student.**

A New Way of Thinking

Educators are asking whether there are tests or alternatives to tests that *truly* assess and evaluate students' growth and progress. There has been a concentrated effort to generate changes in testing to show authentic growth and progress.

Changing tests, however, will not accomplish what is needed. What *is* needed is a change of perspective concerning assessment and evaluation. Classroom teachers are the ones who will bring this new perspective into place. Educators throughout the world, especially those in New Zealand, Australia, Canada, and Great Britain, have taken the lead in pursuing this perspective.

This change of perspective asks . . .

❑ that we see what children *are* doing rather than what they are not doing.

❑ that we understand children learn and progress developmentally and uniquely, not by grade level.

❑ that assessment and evaluation match instruction in the classroom, with the teacher and student as the primary evaluators.

❑ that the progress of a child is documented over time and based upon a variety of evidence rather than on a test.

❑ that we find other ways to show growth rather than rely on numerical summaries.

The educational system has allowed measures outside the classroom to determine the growth and progress of students.

Notes

3. The Basic Principles of Assessment and Evaluation

Assessment refers to the gathering of information, or data collecting. Evaluation refers to the process of examining the evidence and finding value in it.

Defining Assessment and Evaluation

Educators often use the two terms *assessment* and *evaluation* interchangeably, but actually they denote two different processes (Traill, 1992 and Anthony, et al., 1991). Assessment refers to the gathering of information, or data collecting. Evaluation refers to the process of examining the evidence and finding value in it. It is here that judgments and interpretations are made on the collected data. Although these two processes are distinct, they are closely related and can happen simultaneously.

The Purpose of Assessment and Evaluation

Assessment and evaluation are deeply intertwined with instruction. Information which shows a student's progress is continually collected, then used to define and change the curriculum. This collection of information and samples is often housed in a portfolio.

Portfolios offer a wonderful visual presentation of a student's capabilities, strengths, weaknesses, accomplishments and progress. There is an awareness of where the child has been, what steps the child has taken, and a sense of where the child is going.

The Basic Principles of Assessment and Evaluation

On the following pages you will find the basic principles of portfolio assessment and evaluation.

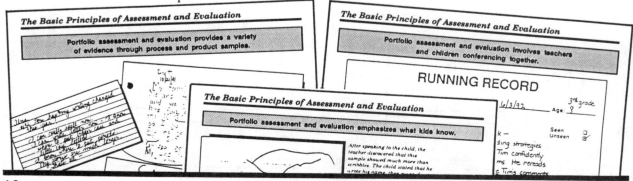

Portfolio assessment and evaluation is ongoing and gathered over time.

Jasonmtfriend$

JAN 17 1990
Dat 1st grade
Published

Josemtfriends

crayons

Lucerosimtfrie

shark

Superman

friend

◄ *First Grade*
Dat is a limited English speaker.
By January he writes simple
frame sentences. There is no
evidence of spaces between words
in his writing.

Dat 2nd grade   4-3-91

Once ther were tow nabor a snel and a spithr. They wre fihtthing ovre the apple tree so they have a contise was a rase. They wer wedy the spithr was in the lide. The snil was last. Then the spithr was

Second Grade
Dat is able to write a story with
a beginning, middle and end.
He spells several high-frequency
words correctly. He now puts
spaces between words.

Nov 12 1991
When I was in a wood I had a shotgun and I was 9 year old and I was going to by a bike for me and I soll two big bear chasing me then I got on the bike and I shote one of the bear the one was left then I cum home me and the bear was still chasing me so I got off my bike and I shot the bear and it was died.

Once upon a time there was a boy named Dai and he always wanted to fight a bear badly. So one morning he went to the woods. Then he saw a bear and he went to the bear. Ant the bear was staring at him and Daien was brave. He is not a chikin he is not afraid of any thing even a monster. Then they started fighting fingting   did the

Third Grade
By October Dat is able to get his
ideas down on paper. As he
writes, he circles words he doesn't
know. He is eager to revise his
work so it can be published.

Portfolio assessment and evaluation embraces different developmental levels.

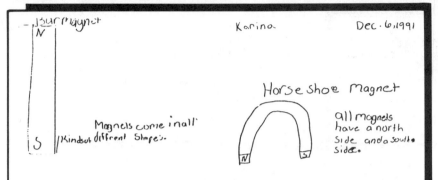

bar magnet   Karina   Dec. 6, 1991

N

S   Magnets come in all
     kinds of diffrent Shape's.

Horse shoe Magnet

all magnets
have a north
Side and a South
Side.

All students participated in the same activity about magnets, yet the samples clearly show the different developmental levels of the students.
Karina combines both illustrations and writing to describe magnets.

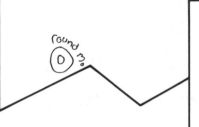

round

Jerod Smith   12\6\9(

1 I know a magnet pulls from a nother magnet because Nort North or south and south don't go together.

O O repeling

3 A magnet can pick up a lot of metel and iron.

2 A magnet is a permit magnet. but the Electro magnet can be tamed on and off.
on and off   permit

4 one of the stronge t magnets is the Electro magnet.

over →

December 6., 1991

Rene   *Written 12/91*

you can mack
you'r Magnet's

Magnet's have
North an South
Poles.

Magne t's cod go Magnet's cod
through your   Pickup metal
Skin.

Jerod is able to communicate in writing his understanding of magnets. He does not rely on illustrations. Rene communicates in simpler sentences, but his illustrations show he understands more than he is able to write. His writing shows that he is still unsure about the purpose of apostrophes.

Portfolio assessment and evaluation matches and guides instruction.

RUNNING RECORD

Name: Tim   Date: 10/5/91   Age: 8   3rd grade

ANALYSIS

		Additional information		Seen ☐
Easy 95–100%	☐			Unseen ☑

Beginning of the year check —
Tim reads at a very early level.
He is developing strategies like repeating
and self-correcting. He needs help
cross-checking cueing systems, and
reading for meaning.

Inst. 90–94% ☑

Hard 50–89% ☐

SCORES

Running Words = $\frac{95}{8}$ = 11.9 = 12 Errors	Error Rate 1:12	% Accuracy 91%	SC 1: Rate

Page	Title and Level Snow Preprimer level	E	SC	Error Analysis	S.C. Analysis
	Jack woke up Saturday morning. He				
	looked out of the window. The ground was	1		ⓜⓢⓥ	
	white. The trees were white. "				
	Jack, "snow."				
	"What did you say?" ask				
	bing his eyes.				
	"It snowed last night.				
	said Jack.				
	Both boys ran to the w				
	"Look at that!" said J				
	Let's get dressed."				
	Jack and John ran into the kitchen.				

Handwritten note card:

10/91
Running record shows Tim doesn't read
for meaning (few self-corrections) &
needs to develop visual (phonic)
decoding skills.

Instructional need — read books that are
"easy" (good picture/clue match) to
build fluency & be successful.

Adapted from *The Early Detection of Reading Difficulties* by Marie Clay

The Basic Principles of Assessment and Evaluation

Portfolio assessment and evaluation is unique to each child.

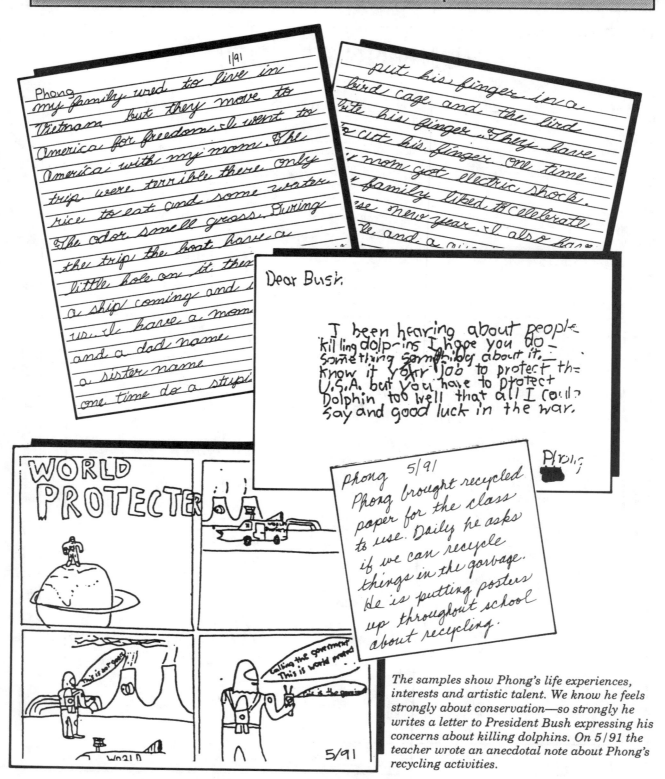

1/91

Phong, my family used to live in Vietnam but they move to America for freedom. I went to America with my mom. The trip were terrible there only rice to eat and some water. The odor smell gross. During the trip the boat have a little hole on it then a ship coming and u. I have a mom and a dad name a sister name one time do a stupi...

put his finger in a bird cage and the bird bite his finger. They have cut his finger one time mom got electric shock. family liked to celebrate new year. I also have and a n...

Dear Bush,

I been hearing about people killing dolpins I hope you do something somthibg about it. I know it your job to protect the U.S.A. but you have to protect Dolphin too well that all I could say and good luck in the war.

Phong

WORLD PROTECTER

5/91

Phong   5/91

Phong brought recycled paper for the class to use. Daily he asks if we can recycle things in the garbage. He is putting posters up throughout school about recycling.

The samples show Phong's life experiences, interests and artistic talent. We know he feels strongly about conservation—so strongly he writes a letter to President Bush expressing his concerns about killing dolphins. On 5/91 the teacher wrote an anecdotal note about Phong's recycling activities.

Portfolio assessment and evaluation emphasizes what kids know.

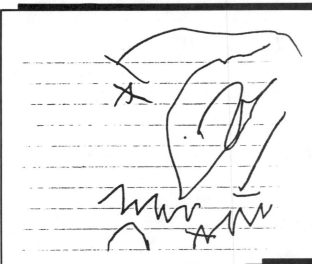

After speaking to the child, the teacher discovered that this sample showed much more than scribbles. The child stated that he wrote his name, then pointed out the letters M A T T.

Here we see the child beginning to use left-to-right progression, along with the use of symbols, to write a story.

Portfolio assessment and evaluation involves teachers
and children conferencing and evaluating together.

RUNNING RECORD

Name: __Tim__   Date: __6/3/92__   Age: __8__   3rd grade

ANALYSIS

Easy 95–100% ☐

Inst. 90–94% ☑

Hard 50–89% ☐

Additional information

End of the year check —
Greatly improved reading strategies
& fluency this year. Tim confidently
uses all cueing systems. He rereads
& self-corrects. See Tim's comments.

Seen ☐
Unseen ☑

SCORES

Running Words = $\frac{99}{8}$ = 12.4 = 12	Error Rate 1:	SC 1: Rate

Errors

Page	Title and Level: Steam Trains — 3rd Grade Basal		S.C. Analysis

The first days of the steam trains
were exciting and dangerous. The trains
looked like big monsters. They threw off
sparks and smoke, ran off the track, and
sometimes even blew up. But everyone
wanted to ride these fast new steam
trains. Soon trains joined the big cities
the east. A great race was started to joi
these cities with the western cities.

Anecdotal Notes 6/3

Teacher: "How has your reading changed this year?"

Tim: (looking at his October running record) "Tell me what I read in October."

Teacher: (reads like Tim did in October) "...Look side John. Come one on..."

Tim: "That doesn't make sense! Reading is supposed to make sense."

Teacher: "I'm glad you know that now."

MSV / MSV

Adapted from *The Early Detection of Reading Difficulties* by Marie Clay

Portfolio assessment and evaluation provides a variety of evidence through process and product samples.

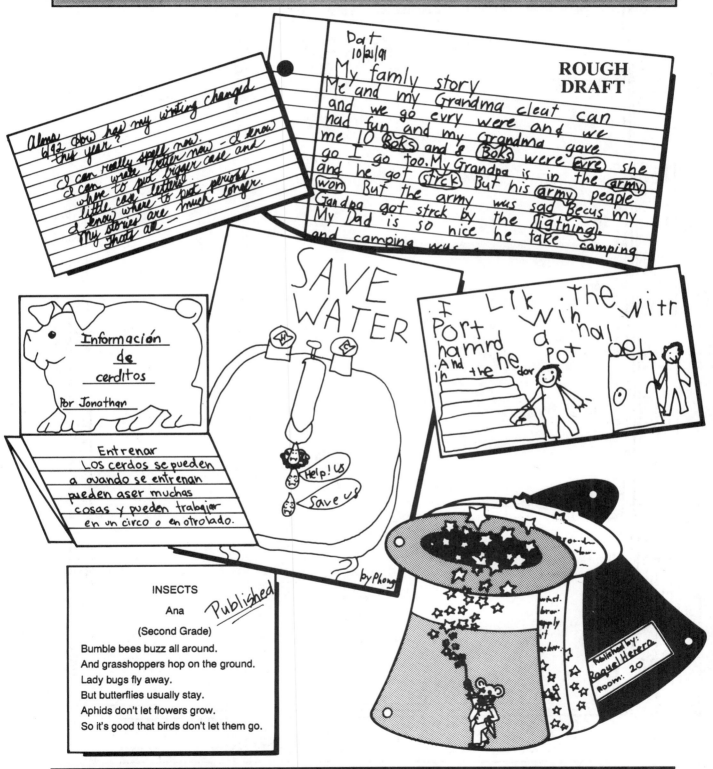

Notes

Part II
Working With Portfolios

4. *Portfolio Essentials*

Process samples are works-in-progress. They show how a student thinks, emphasizing strategies and procedures used.

Product samples are finished, revised works. They show a student's strengths and achievements.

What is a portfolio?

A portfolio is a collection of . . .

- student process samples
- student product samples
- teacher observations
- information gathered through assessment and evaluation strategies
- parent comments

Portfolios come in many sizes and shapes—there is no standard container. Some teachers use cardboard boxes, scrapbooks, or three-ring binders. Most teachers use a file folder or an accordion-type folder for each student. This is an excellent way to organize samples and records and is easily accessible to both student and teacher.

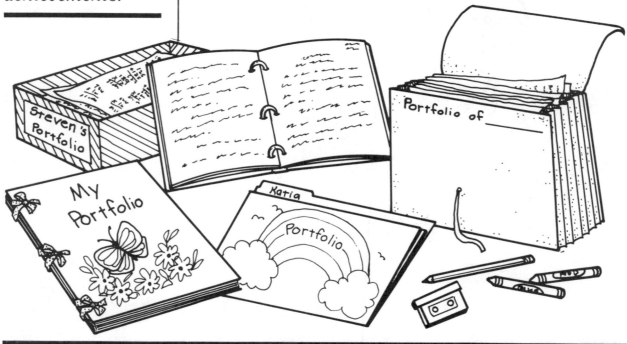

Over time, the portfolio builds up into a very rich data bank. When choosing a way to store gathered information, a school-wide implementation of portfolios should be considered. Ideally, each year selected samples are passed on to the next grade level. Questions the school staff might ask are:

- ❏ Is there enough room for each child's samples from kindergarten through sixth grade?

- ❏ Can the portfolio size be managed easily as it passes through the grade levels?

- ❏ Is the portfolio workable for both students and teacher in the classroom?

- ❏ Does the portfolio hold all the samples — tapes, odd-sized papers, artwork?

Types of Portfolios

There are many types of portfolios that can be used in the classroom, and each has its advantages and disadvantages. Three of the most common are explained on the following pages. Teachers should explore and find out which type works best for them, their students and parents.

The Working Portfolio

The working portfolio is one in which the teacher and child assess and evaluate together. The student chooses samples that show his/her growth, parents contribute comments, and the teacher adds samples and other records. All perspectives (student, teacher and parent) are included to present a realistic picture.

The strength of this type of portfolio is that it presents the most accurate picture of the child's progress. **It tells the whole story of the child—with process and product samples showing daily progress.** It could be very easy, however, for the teacher to dominate this type of portfolio. It is important to keep the portfolio in a central place for equal access to ensure the child's involvement and sense of ownership.

The working portfolio tells the whole story of the child.

Teacher and Student Assessment		Teacher and Student Evaluation

Barbara

Process samples →

Product samples →

TEACHER CHOICE	STUDENT CHOICE
Running Records	Projects
Conference Records	Published Books
Reading Inventory	Photographs
Writing Inventory	Computer Disk of Writing
Student Work Samples	Math Journal Samples
Progress Checks	Writing Samples
Parent Survey	Reading Responses
Attitude Inventory	Reflections

Wealth of information to guide instruction →

Knowledge of the child's strengths →

Evidence of child's self-evaluative strategies →

The Showcase Portfolio

The showcase portfolio is modeled after an artist's portfolio, which is developed to show the artist's best work. It is limited in that it houses only the child's very *best* work—process pieces are not usually included.

This portfolio is powerful because children are motivated to publish books and to develop projects and other exhibitions of their best work and abilities. Here the student has total ownership. It is difficult, however, to guide instruction from the information gathered for this portfolio. The span of the child's day-to-day performance is not usually presented in a showcase portfolio.

When presented with this type of portfolio, parents are very excited and impressed with their child's work. It is then difficult for them to understand the needs of their child because the portfolio samples do not represent the full picture.

The showcase portfolio is modeled after an artist's portfolio, which is developed to show the artist's best work.

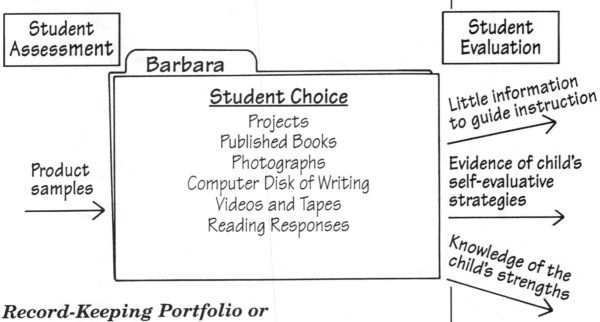

Student Assessment

Barbara

Student Choice
Projects
Published Books
Photographs
Computer Disk of Writing
Videos and Tapes
Reading Responses

Product samples

Student Evaluation

Little information to guide instruction

Evidence of child's self-evaluative strategies

Knowledge of the child's strengths

Record-Keeping Portfolio or Teacher Portfolio

Those teachers using only a showcase portfolio often develop a record-keeping portfolio. In it the teacher keeps necessary assessment and evaluation samples and records not chosen by the student for the showcase portfolio. Also, districts may ask for certain tests to be kept in a portfolio and some teachers may prefer to keep these in the record-keeping portfolio.

When does a teacher find time for portfolios?

Portfolio assessment and evaluation is *not* something to add to the responsibility of the teaching day. It is *not* an added record-keeping activity. In a classroom full of meaningful hands-on experiences where children are responsible learners, the teacher has the opportunity to assess and evaluate during the school day. Teachers successful with portfolios schedule specific times in their daily routine to observe, collect and evaluate. Within a balanced literacy program (chapter 7), assessment and evaluation are seen as a crucial part of daily occurrences.

How are portfolios developed?

The teacher and student (and often parents) are involved in portfolio development. As a teacher observes, she collects samples, anecdotal records and evidence of progress made. Students also choose samples, reflect on their work, and share their achievements. In order to be effective, teachers need to become familiar with the methods of assessing, evaluating and recording data found in chapter 5.

The following are suggested steps for involving children and their parents in the evaluation process:

✎ The student chooses a sample and reviews it with a peer.

✎ The student shares the sample with the class.

✎ The student reflects and writes about why he/she chose the sample and explains its value.

✎ The student takes the sample home for parents' comments and reflections. (See parent forms on pages 118 and 120.)

✎ The student puts the sample in the portfolio so the teacher can write a formal evaluation.

Remember! This is a new experience for parents and students. When they are asked to become part of the assessment and evaluation process, the mystery is taken out of evaluation, grades and report cards.

As children take responsibility for their own learning, they begin to understand how to help themselves.

Where are portfolios developed?

Samples are developed primarily in the classroom and are a vital part of classroom instruction. This type of assessment involves asking students questions, recording observations, and guiding children in self-evaluation—strategies that can only be implemented within the context of the classroom.

Who is involved in portfolios?

The child and the teacher should be involved with the ongoing development of the portfolio. Student self-evaluation is a *major* component of portfolio assessment and evaluation. Parents are involved through their comments, suggestions and classroom visits.

The student's role in portfolio development

Student self-evaluation is a major component in portfolio development. Involving students in the assessment and evaluation process allows them to own their learning.

Traditionally students ask, *How long should my paper be?* or *How can I get an A?* When a child is asked to decide what is his best work, he starts by asking these questions of himself instead of the teacher. Thus students grow in their ability to make decisions and develop an increasing capacity to take responsibility for their learning.

The teacher, as a facilitator, assists children in choosing their best work, and asks them to reflect on its value and share what it tells about their learning. An effective strategy to help students move into self-evaluation is through questioning. Some questions include:

❑ Why did you choose this sample?

❑ What do you think is especially strong about your _____?

❑ How does this sample compare with other samples you've written this year?

> *Students involved with assessment and evaluation grow in their ability to make decisions and develop an increasing capacity to take responsibility for their learning.*

Alma
6/92 How does this sample compare with other samples you've written this year?

I can write better now – I know where to put bigger case and little case letters. I know where to put periods.
My stories are much longer.
I can really spell now.
    That's all —

❑ Which piece do you think is the very best? What makes it the best?

❑ How has your _____ changed this year?

Veronica
6/92 How has your writing changed this year?

I really needed glasses. I have gotten better since I have glasses. I learned to write little. I used to write messy, now I write pretty. It's weird seeing how I used to write.

Carlos
6/92 How has your writing changed this year?

I used to capitalize in the middle of a word.
I didn't use periods and made a lot of spelling mistakes.
My stories are much more exciting now.
I like writing a lot more now.

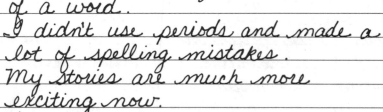

- ❏ How do you think you could make your _____ better?
- ❏ What helps you understand better?
- ❏ What makes learning hard for you?
- ❏ How do these samples show how your _____ has grown?

I do a lot more writing now.

> Simon
> 6/92 How do these samples show how your work has grown?
>
> I am starting to write comedy now.
> I do a lot more writing now.
> I am writing realistic fiction too.
> Before, I just wrote fiction.
> It's the same in capitals, periods and spelling.

Children's self evaluation does not happen overnight. It takes time for students to develop their decision-making skills and their ability to reflect. They need to gain confidence in becoming critics of their own work.

Give children experiences with evaluating literature and other student's writing to help them develop their own evaluative criteria. Model questioning for students so they begin to question themselves in a similar manner. Give positive input and accept the approximations a student makes.

The Student's Role (cont.)

As children take responsibility for their own learning, they begin to understand the process and how to help themselves. Teachers often give forms to students to help them evaluate their learning (page 119). However, when students are encouraged to reflect on their learning by writing about it, they provide more information about their attitude, style of learning, and self-concept.

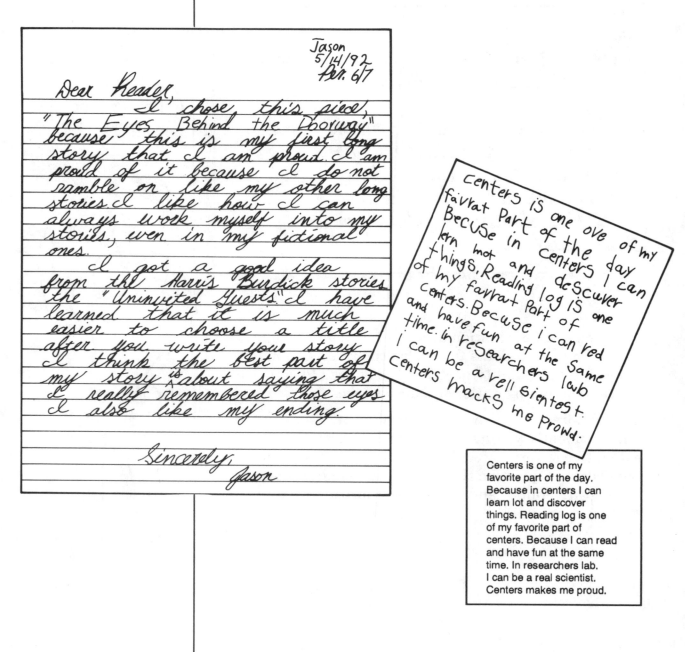

Jason
5/14/92
Per. 6/7

Dear Reader,

I chose this piece, "The Eyes Behind the Doorway" because this is my first long story that I am proud. I am proud of it because I do not ramble on, like my other long stories. I like how I can always work myself into my stories, even in my fictional ones.

I got a good idea from the Harris Burdick stories the "Uninvited Guests." I have learned that it is much easier to choose a title after you write your story. I think the best part of my story is about saying that I really remembered those eyes. I also like my ending.

Sincerely,
Jason

Centers is one of my favorite part of the day. Because in centers I can learn lot and discover things. Reading log is one of my favorite part of centers. Because I can read and have fun at the same time. In researchers lab. I can be a real scientist. Centers makes me proud.

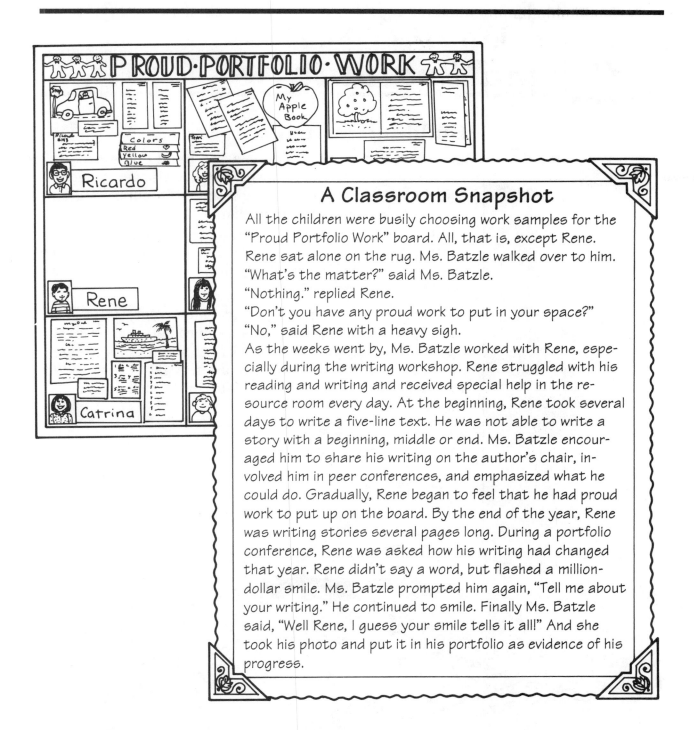

A Classroom Snapshot

All the children were busily choosing work samples for the "Proud Portfolio Work" board. All, that is, except Rene. Rene sat alone on the rug. Ms. Batzle walked over to him.

"What's the matter?" said Ms. Batzle.

"Nothing." replied Rene.

"Don't you have any proud work to put in your space?"

"No," said Rene with a heavy sigh.

As the weeks went by, Ms. Batzle worked with Rene, especially during the writing workshop. Rene struggled with his reading and writing and received special help in the resource room every day. At the beginning, Rene took several days to write a five-line text. He was not able to write a story with a beginning, middle or end. Ms. Batzle encouraged him to share his writing on the author's chair, involved him in peer conferences, and emphasized what he could do. Gradually, Rene began to feel that he had proud work to put up on the board. By the end of the year, Rene was writing stories several pages long. During a portfolio conference, Rene was asked how his writing had changed that year. Rene didn't say a word, but flashed a million-dollar smile. Ms. Batzle prompted him again, "Tell me about your writing." He continued to smile. Finally Ms. Batzle said, "Well Rene, I guess your smile tells it all!" And she took his photo and put it in his portfolio as evidence of his progress.

To help students develop their evaluative judgments, give each child a block of space on a bulletin board titled *Proud Portfolio Work*. Ask the child to find samples to display in the space, and share in writing why he/she chose those samples. This is crucial to establishing the student's ownership. If a child has difficulty making decisions about which sample to choose, ask him or her to work with another student.

5. Ways to Assess and Evaluate

Building Portfolios

As you work towards portfolio assessment and evaluation it is important for you to develop at a comfortable pace. You may already have the beginnings of a portfolio collection. For example, you are probably keeping student creative writing samples. Take the next step and review a sample with the student author. Analyze the sample, then use all this information to help determine future instruction.

When collecting information and samples for portfolio development there should be a balance between process and product samples. It is important to understand the process a child goes through in order to get to the product. Product and process samples yield different kinds of information.

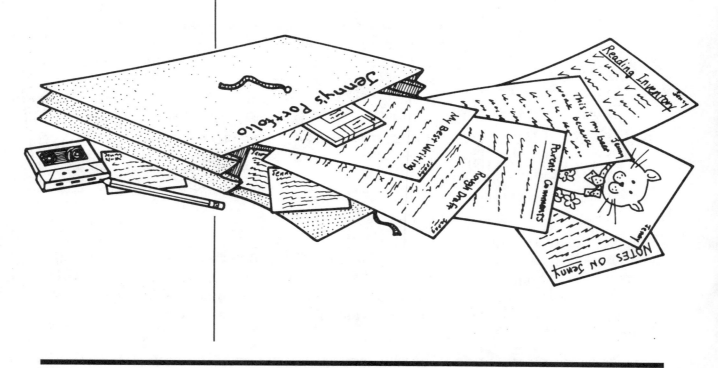

Here is an overview of the *possible* measures and samples to include in a portfolio. For more detailed information about the items, refer to the pages following the outline.

I. Required Tests and Accountability Measures (page 36)
- ❏ Standardized Tests
- ❏ Minimum Competency Tests
- ❏ Criterion-Referenced Tests
- ❏ Chapter or Unit Tests

II. Samples Across the Curriculum (page 36)
- ❏ Language Arts
  - ✓ Reading Responses
  - ✓ Reading Logs
  - ✓ Home Reading Logs
  - ✓ Oral Reading Tapes
  - ✓ Writing Folders
  - ✓ Writing Samples
  - ✓ Spelling Work
- ❏ Math
- ❏ Fine Arts
- ❏ Content Areas

III. Teacher Observations and Measures (page 43)
- ❏ Kid Watching and Anecdotal Records
- ❏ Running Records
- ❏ Retellings
- ❏ Progress Checks
- ❏ Teacher-made Tests
- ❏ Rubrics
- ❏ Conference Records
- ❏ Summary of Findings

IV. Inventories and Other Forms (page 55)
- ❏ Reading Inventory
- ❏ Informal Reading Inventory
- ❏ Writing Inventory
- ❏ Parent Surveys, Comments and Evaluations

V. Additional Items (page 56)
- ❏ Cassette or Photo of Drama Presentations
- ❏ Oral Presentation, Booktalk
- ❏ Oral Language Inventory
- ❏ Oral "publishing"

I. Required Tests and Accountability Measures

There are many pressures for district accountability that can only be answered by administering standardized tests and district or grade level exams. What we must realize, however, is that these measures are not the most meaningful to the teacher in guiding instruction.

II. Samples Across the Curriculum

Collect both process and product samples from all curricular areas. Date each sample chosen for the portfolio. Write an anecdotal note explaining it, where it was collected, and other important data. If you do not want to write on the sample itself, write on a sticky note, label or index card, and attach this to the sample.

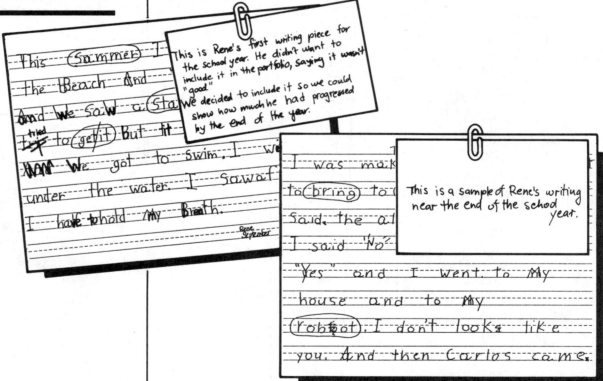

When the child chooses a sample, she can write or dictate why she chose it and what it shows about her progress (see page 118). The child's evaluation is important information which can be passed along to the next teacher.

❏ Language Arts

✓ Reading Responses

Children's responses to whole group and small group reading provide a wealth of information. There are many types of reading responses students can do—webbing, book buddy journals, double entry journals, and story maps. These are good ways to evaluate a child's ability to summarize and to reflect on what he reads. After reading a text, a child might respond in the following ways.

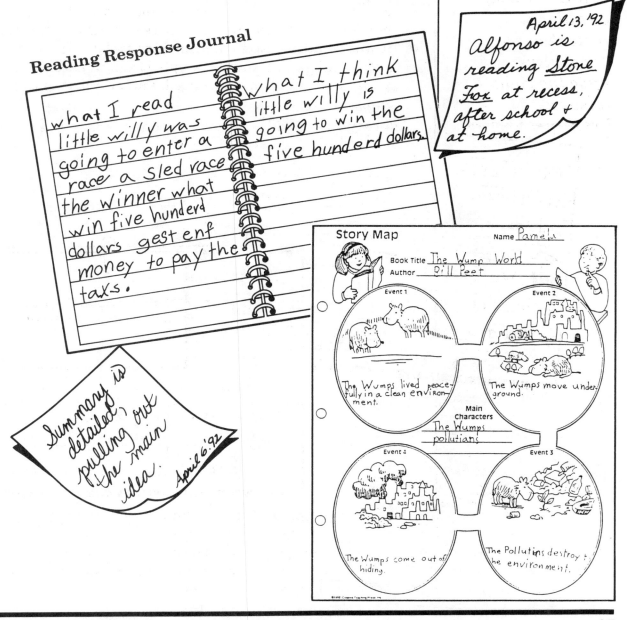

Reading Response Journal

what I read little willy was going to enter a sled race the winner what win five hunderd dollars gest enf money to pay the taxs.

what I think little willy is going to win the five hunderd dollars.

April 13, '92
Alfonso is reading _Stone Fox_ at recess, after school + at home.

Summary is detailed, pulling out the main idea. April 6 '92

Story Map   Name Pamela

Book Title The Wump World
Author Bill Peet

Event 1 — The Wumps lived peacefully in a clean environment.

Event 2 — The Wumps move underground.

Main Characters — The Wumps pollutians

Event 4 — The Wumps come out of hiding.

Event 3 — The Pollutins destroy the environment.

✓ Reading Logs

Students should keep a log of the books they read throughout the year (page 103). Early readers can write the name of the book and the author. Fluent readers record the name of the book, the author, and the genre. These logs provide information on the independent reading level of each child and the variety of books chosen.

The date the child starts and finishes a book may indicate interest in the book, fluency level and reading speed. A teacher gains additional insights by discussing the book with the child.

✓ Home Reading Logs

A home reading log (page 104) provides information about a child's access to books outside school. It can tell a teacher about the child's personal book collection, library visits, and whether someone reads to the child at home.

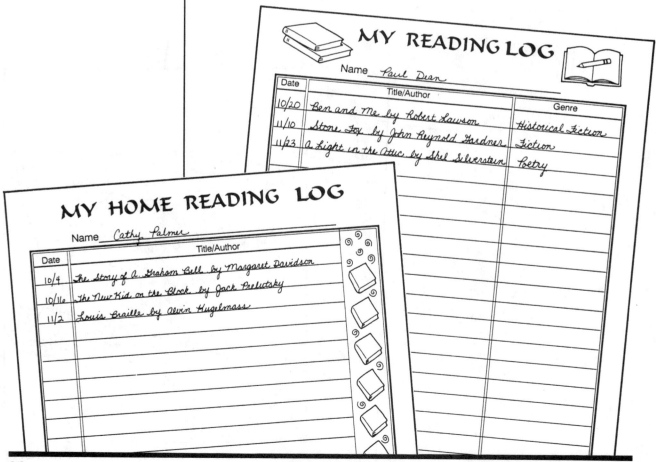

MY READING LOG

Name _Paul Dean_

Date	Title/Author	Genre
10/20	Ben and Me by Robert Lawson	Historical Fiction
11/10	Stone Fox by John Reynold Gardner	Fiction
11/23	A Light in the Attic by Shel Silverstein	Poetry

MY HOME READING LOG

Name _Cathy Palmer_

Date	Title/Author
10/4	The Story of A. Graham Bell by Margaret Davidson
10/16	The New Kid on the Block by Jack Prelutsky
11/2	Louis Braille by Alvin Hugelmass

✓ Oral Reading Tapes

Tape a child's reading two to three times a year as a record of developing fluency. Although recommended by many teachers, taping children's oral reading seems to provide less information to guide instruction than other evaluative tools like running records (pages 48–49).

✓ Writing Folders

Keep a child's daily writing in a file folder, then put significant samples into the portfolio. Have the child monitor and record all new learnings and understandings developed through writing. Review these during conferences and place them in the portfolio. Keep a record in the portfolio of the child's published pieces (page 105). This will give you information about the genre of books published, as well as the number of writing pieces published that year. A cumulative personal word bank can be kept in the folder. This provides a record of the words a child is learning to spell.

✓ Writing Samples

Every month collect and date writing samples. Collect writing from all genres in order to understand the strengths and needs of the writer. Writing samples written in journals, content area writing, and reading responses are all important data. A student's unique writing process should be represented, including the prewriting strategies used, rough draft, revision (if any), a record of the content of conferences (page 115), and the published text. Some teachers prefer to return original samples to students and make copies to keep in the portfolios.

After collecting a sample, discuss it with the child. Many times teachers make assumptions about the writing that are different from what the child had in mind. Start with the child talking about the sample. Listen to what the child says about it and what her intentions and goals were.

✓ Spelling Work

Spelling progress is assessed through writing samples collected through the year. By comparing the child's spelling to the developmental stages (pages 82–86), you can evaluate movement towards conventional spelling. Record this information on the writing inventory (pages 106–109), along with other behaviors related to spelling, like use of resources and the ability to identify misspelled words.

❏ Math

Collect progress checks of students' computational skills, along with samples showing students' problem-solving strategies. Keeping a math journal is an excellent way for a student to respond daily to problem-solving situations. The student's response through drawings, writings, and computations shows thinking processes and the ability to apply computational skills.

What I Know about Frations

Hands on Math

Prefracto
Pam
05-07-17
10-19-92

The things I Know about Frations is I know that $\frac{1}{2}$ is =to 50¢ of a dollar because see if you have $1.00 it is 100 pennies and if you split that into 2 groups it is 50¢. And $\frac{3}{4}$ on a clock is 45 min because it isn't quite 1 hour bun it's close $\frac{4}{4}$ is one full hour. Anything with the same number is one full thing heres on exampls

⊕ = 4/4
⊕ = ½ or ⅘
⊕ = ¼

Cameron
10-18-92
05-07-04

Prefraction

Fractions

Fractions are a problem that is split in half. For example say you have a bag of chips and you don't want them, but two of your friends do so you split the chips in half you give one friend one half you give the other a nother? half. Fractions are problems you split in half or in many other ways. Sometimes you can make fractions fair and sometimes you don't always make them fair. Fractions are real easy to me and ll think everyone else.

❏ Fine Arts

Children's art samples often show developmental growth, especially in young children. Art samples display the unique talents of children. Video-tape performances like Reader's Theater, plays, and puppet shows. Record songs or "oral publishing" on cassette tapes.

❑ Content Areas

When starting a theme students record in their learning logs what they know about the theme, questions they have, and ideas of what they want to learn. As the theme progresses, students take notes on their reading and their learning experiences. This becomes a continuous record of learning throughout the theme. Projects like research reports, displays, published books, and plays become culminating evidences of a student's learning.

If projects won't fit in the portfolio, take photographs of them. A photograph of a cooperative project provides a sample for each member's portfolio. Each student should reflect in writing what was learned in the process of developing the project.

When Rocio started the Ecosystem theme in January, she knew very little. In a progress check in April, she was asked to write about what she had learned.

Angelica shows how much she learned from April to May. Note how her sentences are now full of information and how her handwriting improved.

III. Teacher Observations and Measures

☐ Kid Watching and Anecdotal Records

In 1978, Yetta Goodman suggested an alternative to testing called *kid watching*. She found that the classroom teacher's informal observation of the child in various situations could provide much more information than standardized tests.

The more a teacher understands children and their language development, the more he/she is able to "catch" the evidence through observation. **Kid watching is at the heart of collecting and building portfolios.** By observing the process a student uses, the teacher gains information about how the student arrives at the product. For example in the classroom snapshot on page 44, the teacher discovers the valuable information that Tim is an auditory learner.

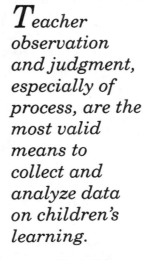

Teacher observation and judgment, especially of process, are the most valid means to collect and analyze data on children's learning.

Regie Routman

Kid watching is done from two viewpoints—involved and objective.

✎ **Involved observations** are done while the teacher instructs and works with students.

✎ **Objective observations** are done as the teacher watches students function and work independently.

A Classroom Snapshot

I observe and take notes on what centers my students choose. I have a classroom that accommodates different styles of learning, so I feel observing a student's choices tells me what kind of learner he or she is. Tim consistently chooses to listen to books and accompanying tapes, and to watch films related to the theme we are studying. He voluntarily brings paper to the listening center to take notes. When we discuss the theme as a whole class, he actively participates and shares information. As an involved observer, I noted his interest in the theme, his ability to share orally with the group, and his competence in collecting and building knowledge on a subject. As an objective observer, I noted the avenue he used to access this information. After seeing this pattern repeated over time, I realized that Tim was an auditory learner. When I asked him to think about his learning at center time and write about it, he wrote the following sample.

Centers
~~Centers~~   I like centers beCus i
luern supting new   a very day. Your poropy
thaking how i luern from centers i luern
from center from wotching and lisining clos ly.
And i am carfoll of my work.

Centers
I like centers because I learn
something new every day.
You're probably thinking how I
learn from centers I learn from
center from watching and
listening closely.
And I am careful of
my work.

Anecdotal Records

Record observations when kid watching by writing anecdotes. Keep in mind, anecdotal records are objective because they report rather than evaluate or interpret.

Learning to take anecdotal records is like developing a new habit. Set aside a specific time in the day to observe and take anecdotal notes. Set a goal for how many students you will observe each day. As you observe and record, mark off student names on a checklist. Within a short time you will find you have written a note for every child in your class. When you have an opportunity, place these notes in the portfolios. Soon this process will become automatic!

Ways to Record Anecdotes

✎ Keep a grid on a clipboard with a square for each student. This is convenient for carrying around the room.

✎ Keep an index card on each student and file it later in the portfolio.

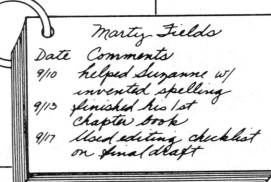

Marty Fields
Date	Comments
9/10	helped Suzanne w/ invented spelling
9/13	finished his 1st chapter book
9/17	Used editing checklist on final draft

Terry Barton
Date	Comments
10/19	- Built a space city with José. Good cooperation.
10/27	- Researched comets in 3 sources.
11/2	- Tape recorded original science fiction story.

✎ Take notes using a calendar. Reserve one space per student. Record observations on sticky notes and attach them to the spaces. As the calendar is filled up with notes, it is easy to see who has not been observed. Later transfer the sticky notes with the information into the portfolios.

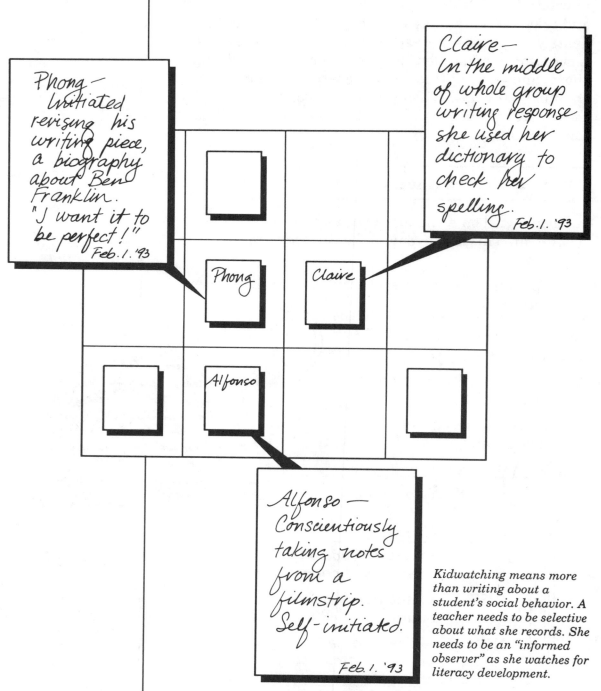

Phong—
Initiated revising his writing piece, a biography about Ben Franklin. "I want it to be perfect!"
Feb. 1. '93

Claire—
In the middle of whole group writing response she used her dictionary to check her spelling.
Feb. 1. '93

Phong

Claire

Alfonso

Alfonso—
Conscientiously taking notes from a filmstrip. Self-initiated.
Feb. 1. '93

Kidwatching means more than writing about a student's social behavior. A teacher needs to be selective about what she records. She needs to be an "informed observer" as she watches for literacy development.

✎ Keep notes in a three-ring binder, with a divider tab for each student. This develops into a diary of the child's progress. This is one of the easiest ways to make anecdotal records a permanent part of the portfolio.

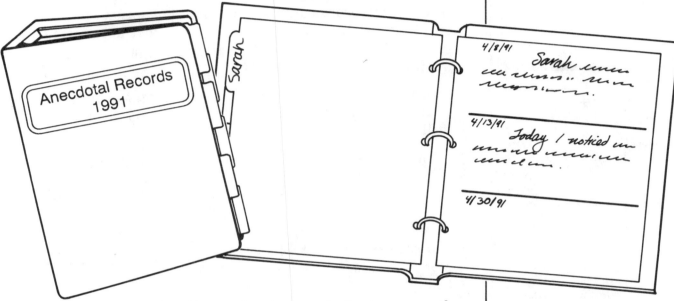

Anecdotal records tell you about your students as no other measure can. Use the writing and reading inventories found in chapter 9 to help you observe and identify developmental stages in language. When you read the anecdotal record, ask yourself these questions:

- What does this information tell me about this child?
- Where is this child along the developmental continuum?
- What does this information tell me about the child's instructional needs?

❏ Running Records

Running records, developed by Marie Clay as part of the Reading Recovery program, help teachers understand the strategies and cueing systems a reader uses. A running record can also provide information for guiding instruction—such as selecting text appropriate for instruction and information for grouping children.

Running records are meant to be done "on the run"—making them possible to do with a classroom full of children.

In a running record the teacher uses certain conventions to record everything a child says and does while reading a sample text of 100–150 words. For developing readers, do running records every 4–6 weeks; for strong readers, every 2–3 months. Running record summaries are kept as a permanent part of a child's portfolio. The following page shows a running record sample.

Running records are meant to be done "on the run."

Although they may seem a bit overwhelming at first, running records are fairly easy to learn, and only require practice on the part of the teacher. The pay-off in gaining evaluative information is well worth the effort put into learning the process.

After analyzing a running record, a teacher determines the instructional level of the text (whether appropriate or too difficult), and what cueing systems the child uses. (For more information on cueing systems, see pages 87–89.)

There are several sources to assist you in doing running records:

- Reading Recovery teachers—trained in many cities in the United States—use running records daily in their program.

- Marie Clay's book, *The Early Detection of Reading Difficulties,* explains how to go about doing running records.

- Rigby Education's two videos by Leanna Traill, *Taking Running Records* and *Using Running Records*, model how to take a running record and analyze children's reading.

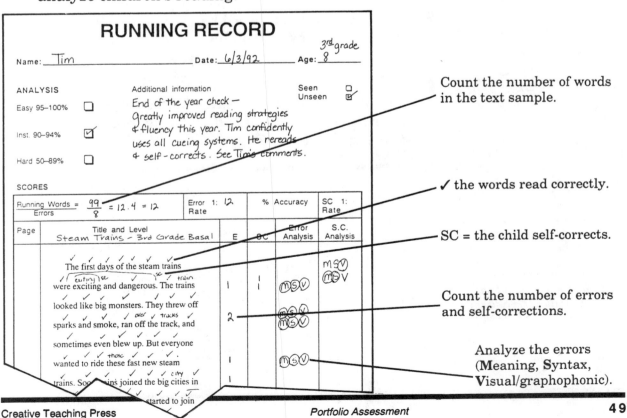

Count the number of words in the text sample.

✓ the words read correctly.

SC = the child self-corrects.

Count the number of errors and self-corrections.

Analyze the errors (**M**eaning, **S**yntax, **V**isual/graphophonic).

❑ Retellings

Retelling is a strategy to accompany running records and help in the evaluation of a child's comprehension. Instead of questioning the student about what he just read, ask him to retell the story orally or in writing as if he were telling it to someone who has never heard it before.

If the child retells in writing, then spelling and grammar data can be evaluated, along with text comprehension, sequencing of ideas, and ability to reconstruct text. For more information on the retelling strategy, read Brown and Cambourne's book *Read and Retell.*

❑ Progress Checks

Progress checks with open formats give children opportunities to show what they have internalized.

Without prompts, questioning, or review, children are able to "show what they know." Ask students to fold a plain white paper into fourths—providing four spaces on each side. Ask students to "show what they know" about a particular theme or unit of study by having them diagram, draw, or write in the spaces.

You might cover up word banks and displays in the room so you have a reliable source of spelling progress, summarizing ability, knowledge and understanding of the subject.

Young children usually draw big pictures to describe their learning. Older children move into diagrams and always ask for more paper!

Here Spencer shows what he knows about dinosaurs—names and some characteristics.

Rather than choose a predetermined answer in a multiple-choice test, Veronica shows what she understands and values from her study of the solar system.

By using progress checks, reviewing a child's learning logs, evaluating projects, and listening to the child's own evaluation of her work, a teacher learns about the child's learning process and has a rich source of data to help understand the child's strengths in a variety of contexts.

Ben Franklin is a printer sintist he made swimming paddle he descover ilicktrsody is lightning and he was born 1706.

In the 1840, people travle with wagin weels becuase they didit have no car in the 1840.

Dat Jan 24 1992 In the 1840 kids don't play with Nintendo and Gameboy they just go out to a tree and made a swing By it are just play with a doll are jump on there bed.

They live ih a log cabin net in a house are a apatmat.

They kill anomals for there dinner and they use bear skin for a Kote.

In the 1840 kids coll the father Pa and they coll the Mother Ma.

In the 1840 the womens and girls can't were pants ohly dris but over here women and girls cuald were pants.

My famly is born in Vietnam but my baby sister is born over here we ackape to get over here.

Dat started speaking English in 1st grade. By 3rd grade he is able to explain history by relating it to his own family.

Jerod   Date January 24, 1992

Betsy Ross
Betsy Ross was the designer of our flag. It took her a long time to finish the flag.

Ben Franklin
Ben Franklin was born in 1706 he ate like we do because he wasn't dive when the Ingalls were.

Little House In The Big Woods The ingalls family ate everyday thay got there milk from the cou Satunda they went to town.

The Long Way To A New Land
The swedish family were in Englen they wanted to go to America it was a trip

hot Do d

Jerod participated in the same theme, but has a different response to history. These two samples demonstrate why multiple choice tests do not always provide a way for a child to "show what he knows."

Teacher-made Tests

When you develop tests, keep in mind the different ways children learn. The tests we use often limit a child to an answer that isn't necessarily *his* answer. When tests are more open-ended, children's responses tell teachers much more about what they are thinking.

Children who use English as a second language often don't perform well on written language tests. But they can show in other ways that they understand a concept. For example, a child using a pocket chart can match animal classification vocabulary with the correct description and animal picture. This method shows what the child knows without requiring her to deal with the added challenge of written language.

Rubrics

A rubric is a scoring guide designed to evaluate a student's performance within a specific curricular area.

In the writing curriculum a rubric could measure the following components of a student's writing:

- Ideas included in the writing
- Organization of the writing
- Word choice used in the writing
- Sentence structure used
- Mechanics found in the writing—punctuation, capitalization, spelling

Once you decide on the components of the rubric, you need to devise a rating scale. Rating scales typically range from 0 to 8, with the largest number indicating an outstanding score. Finally, for each score, write the criteria which will be used to judge the child's writing.

> *Children who use English as a second language can show that they understand a concept.*

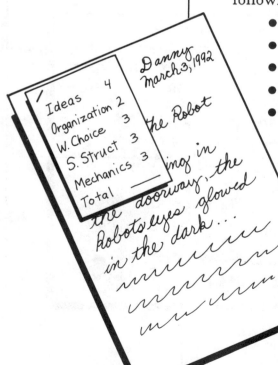

The purpose of rubric scoring is to help teachers clarify their goals, process instruction, and involve students in self-evaluation.

One way to assure that a rubric is focused on students is to create the rubric *with students*. This is an instructional technique in and of itself, requiring students to develop vocabulary and engage in determining overall goals.

The following chart is an example of a teacher-created rubric for a creative writing assignment.

Evaluating Creative Writing

	Ideas	Organization	Word Choice	Sentence Structure	Mechanics
4	Fresh, original Focuses on topic Supporting details	Ideas connected Strong beginning, middle, end Sequenced & logical	Wide variety used Consistent and appropriate usage Words "enhance" ideas	Clearly written Complete sentences Variety of sentence length	Few or no errors
3	Some original ideas General focus on topic Most supporting details included	Most ideas connected Good beginning, middle, end Most ideas sequenced & logical	Some variety Mostly consistent and appropriate Words generally support ideas	Most sentences clearly written Simple sentences Some variety of length	Some errors
2	Few original ideas Moves away from focus Few supporting details	Some ideas connected Attempts beginning, middle, end Not always sequenced & logical	Common word choice Some appropriate word choices Little use of descriptive words	Some unclear sentences Run-on, fragmented, sentences Little variety	Many errors
1	Incomplete ideas Unfocused Lacks details	Few ideas connected Lacks beginning, middle, end Little sequence & logic	Limited word choice Inappropriate word choices No atempt at descriptive words	Sentences not clear Frequent fragmented sentences No variety	Serious errors No variety
0	No attempt	No attempt	No attempt	No attempt	No attempt

❑ Conference Records

Conference records are a working part of the portfolio. These are records of observed strengths and needs, discussion highlights, and decisions made jointly by the child and the teacher.

Records should be written weekly as you conference with children. Make copies of the conference record form on page 115. For reading conferences use one color paper; for writing conferences use another color.

❑ Summary of Findings

This summary of a child's growth throughout the year is significant information. It is important to include the summary (page 116) for the student's next teacher.

When using portfolios, there is an opportunity to build a long-term view of the child's development. As you review the portfolio contents, write a summary. Reflect on the child's overall progress. Include pertinent data on how the child goes about writing. Think about the child's reading strategies, his learning preferences and attitudes, and his work habits.

The summary should emphasize what the child **can** do. Pull all the threads of information together and focus on the changes and growth the child has made.

Student Portfolio Summary

School Year __1991__ Student's Name __Lucero__

Date/Grade	Summary
6/4 3rd	Comes from a Spanish-speaking home. ⊘ + letters in Spanish to take home. Publi⊘ English at home to bring to school.
	Easily reads + comprehends 3rd grade Reading _Mrs. Piggle Wiggle_ by choi⊘ to discuss what she reads.
	Has difficulty printing neatly (word she writes fast). Grammar convent⊘ good stories with beginning, middl⊘
	Able to apply computational skill⊘

Conference Record

Name __Vanessa__   Date __3/18/92__

Reading/Writing	Observations	Instructional Need/Goal
Rdg.	_The Wump World_ _Strega Nona_ } can identify main characters. No problem summarizing the stories. Intends to visit library + find books by same author	Help her choose what she calls "grown-up" books for her independent reading.
Rdg.	_Two Bad Ants_ - told me the story + setting from the ants perspective. Enjoyed the story. Doing an excellent job with characterization + point of view.	Help her find more Bill Peet books.

IV. Inventories and Other Forms

Inventories can be overwhelming if a teacher tries to complete them all at the same time! It is highly recommended that you adapt an inventory to your own needs. When you do this, the inventory becomes familiar to you and relevant to your teaching situation. The most effective way to use an inventory is to know it well and fill it in as you collect the evidence. Inventories are also helpful in directing your kid watching. They help to empower teachers by telling them what to look for.

❏ Reading Inventory

A Reading Inventory (pages 99–101) shows a child's progress on a developmental continuum. Developmental markers, which show patterns of growth, are observed and recorded and become a permanent part of the child's portfolio. A Reading Inventory can also be used to help a teacher's observations. For information about development in writing, spelling, and reading see chapter 8.

❏ Informal Reading Inventory

If you need a grade level measure for reading, you might use an Informal Reading Inventory (IRI) to help determine a child's instructional reading level. IRIs are often found in the basal reading series. They consist of a graded word list, and paragraph selections with comprehension questions. You can also use running records on these graded pieces of text.

The text on an informal reading inventory has no picture-cue information. Beginning readers may not be able to read the text, and the background information needed for comprehension may not be appropriate for all students.

❑ Writing Inventory

There are several ways to evaluate writing. A developmental inventory, like those on pages 106–109, shows progress along a continuum. This type of evaluation becomes a record of a child's pattern of growth and development. The inventory is a list of developmental markers—the teacher records the date and her comments when she sees the behavior. The most effective way to use an inventory is to record the behavior when you observe it or when it is evidenced through samples in the classroom. The inventory is kept in the portfolio year after year for other teachers to see. The inventory is not meant to be taken home by the teacher and filled out like a checklist before report card conferences with parents. It is easily managed in the classroom when you conference with students.

❑ Parent Surveys, Comments and Evaluations

We need to provide opportunities for parents to become involved in their child's literacy. Parental input is encouraged and appreciated. Parent surveys, comments, and evaluations (page 117) provide you with valuable information.

V. Additional Items

Additional items for a student portfolio include cassettes, photos, and documentation of oral presentations. Tape a booktalk and keep the script with comments attached. Student and teacher evaluations of oral language inventories and oral "publishing" are also valuable tools in evaluation.

Notes

6. *What to Do With Portfolios*

Organizing Portfolios

In a school-wide implementation, teachers and principal collectively decide what needs to be evaluated and what core samples should be put in the portfolios. These decisions are ideally based upon the profile of students in the school.

Teachers need the autonomy to choose what is relevant and useful to them. They can make or adapt their own evaluative inventories and measures.

The core group of assessment samples and evaluative measures go into a child's portfolio. Students and teachers then make decisions on additional samples to add to the portfolio.

Passing on Portfolios

A teacher needs to review any portfolios passed on to her. Look for patterns of learning, accomplishments, a positive sense of the child, and the strategies used in reading and writing. This provides a wealth of information for the beginning of the school year. You won't have to play the guessing game and take two months to get to know the child. You already have some diagnostic information.

*T*he core group of assessment samples and evaluative measures go into a child's portfolio.

If portfolios are not available, then diagnostic work needs to be done. By following the methods for assessment and evaluation suggested in this book, a portfolio can be started. Passing along *all* of the samples would not be practical for teachers in the years to come because the portfolio would be too cumbersome.

As a portfolio is developed throughout the school year, it becomes thick with a rich collection of authentic samples. When the school year comes to a close, select the most important pieces to pass on to the next teacher. These may include:

Writing samples from the beginning and end of the year

The child's choice of two most important pieces

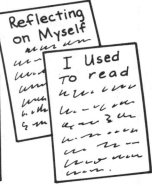

A few of the child's self-evaluative reflections

An additional sample of a project or published book, chosen by the child

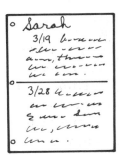

Anecdotal records or a summary of them

Writing and reading inventories from previous grades

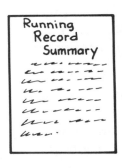

A summary of running records

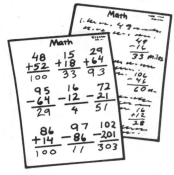

Math—a computational and a problem-solving sample

A teacher-made test

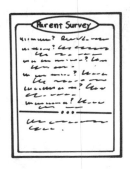

Parent surveys

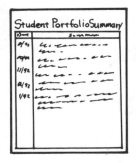

A portfolio summary

A photo of a painting or a drama performance

Portfolios and Report Cards

Putting portfolios and report cards together is like mixing oil and water. When translating portfolio contents and comments into report card grades, it helps to remember that grades rate students on a curve and portfolios allow us to see individuals on a developmental continuum.

But report cards are a reality in most schools. So before you put samples into the portfolios, periodically look at all the samples from the class. By looking holistically at all of them, it is possible to lay them out in *A, B, C* categories. Rubrics (pages 52–53), can also be used for this purpose. Grades should not become a part of the portfolio. A portfolio should be a celebration of the child's unique abilities, achievements, and progress displayed through authentic samples rather than labeled with a grade.

Teachers are trying to change report cards so they match the kind of assessment and evaluation methods implemented in their classroom. These new report cards would tell parents what a grade *really* means, with portfolio contents to tangibly support the grade.

As teachers become more comfortable with anecdotal reporting, they may want to move to anecdotal progress reports as the most accurate way to tell the whole story of the child.

A portfolio should be a celebration of the child's unique abilities, achievements, and progress, displayed through authentic samples.

Reporting to Parents

Teachers should expect parents to question the validity of this new type of assessment, and parents need to be *educated* in order to understand its value. As parents become involved and watch their child participate in self-evaluation, they become supportive of this way of valuing the child. They also appreciate the individualized time spent with their child.

Send home a parent letter at the beginning of the year to let parents know that a lot of the work children produce in the classroom will be saved in portfolios. Describe a portfolio, and define its purpose. Encourage parents to periodically come in and review their child's portfolio. Let them know samples will be sent home for their comments, then returned to the portfolio.

At back-to-school night, once again describe the purpose and principles of portfolio assessment and evaluation. During the first parent conference, ask the parents to fill out and discuss the parent survey (page 117) *with you*. This gives you information about what is happening at home. Show parents the child's portfolio.

As you work through the year, ask the child to take home and show the portfolio samples (or copies of samples) to his parents. Ask him to participate in the parent conference. The child's growth and enthusiasm will speak for itself.

*P*arents need to be educated in order to understand the value of portfolio assessment and evaluation.

A Classroom Snapshot

Alma was used to accompanying her mother to parent conferences. It was important—she was the translator! Ms. B. pulled out Alma's portfolio. Alma smiled. Ms. B. asked, "Would you like to show your mother your portfolio?" Alma nodded. As she pulled out the samples she felt were significant, she laid them out in order—a first, second, and third grade writing sample.

Alma looked at the samples and exclaimed, "See!" She smiled proudly as she looked at her mother, then turned to Ms. B. "Do you think you could take down the big book on the bulletin board and put my writings up there? All of them!"

Notes

Part III

Portfolios in Context

7. Portfolio Assessment and a Balanced Literacy Program

Assessment and evaluation go hand in hand with classroom instruction. For evaluation to be authentic it must take place in the classroom, within the context of a balanced literacy program.

In a balanced literacy program there are three main components. All three components interact and work together.

A Balanced Literacy Program

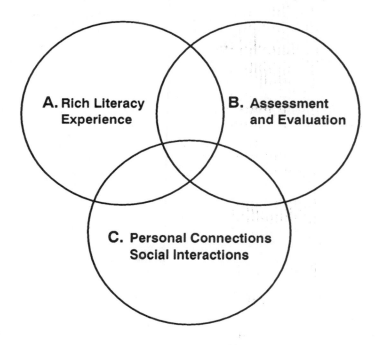

A. Rich Literacy Experience

B. Assessment and Evaluation

C. Personal Connections Social Interactions

A. Rich Literacy Experience

A rich literacy experience is one in which children are immersed in the enjoyment and purposeful use of books. Children develop independent reading and writing strategies through shared reading (whole group), personalized reading (in small groups and independently), writing workshop and read-alouds. Books for all these purposes are displayed throughout the room.

A rich literacy classroom environment surrounds children with a variety of reading and writing experiences and examples. This type of print-rich classroom includes the following:

Creation Station

This is the place where a child's creativity can flow in response to experiences with literature. A variety of arts and crafts materials are available for children.

Writing Center

Stock this area with paper in different sizes and shapes so young authors can publish books, and work on self-editing checklists and writing folders. Include word banks and several types of dictionaries. A post office area encourages children to communicate in writing.

The Word Center

Using dictionaries and thesauruses, a student works on developing word strategies and a personal word bank.

Author's Chair

An author's chair awaits a special writer. The child sits in this place of honor and shares her writing with the class.

In a classroom with a balanced literacy program the children are actively involved, allowing the teacher time to work with small groups and gather information for evaluation.

Science Center

This research lab displays equipment, scientific diagrams, nonfiction texts related to a theme, learning logs or journals to record observations, and hands-on experiments.

Math Center

This center contains related literature, math materials, games, and math manipulatives.

Listening Center

In the listening center there are books with accompanying tapes, blank tapes for children to record their own stories, and a projector for viewing filmstrips.

Drama Center

At the drama center, young actors are enticed to retell favorite stories through puppetry and role playing.

Research Area

This area houses nonfiction and resource books, maps, and almanacs for digging up information. This is the place where children find the answers to their questions.

Large Group Area

The classroom has an area where children can read in a whole group. This area can be used for calendar and pocket chart activities and group discussions.

Conference Table

This becomes a focal point in the classroom where teacher and students have conversations, read, write and evaluate together. The portfolios are placed here so everyone has access to them.

Portfolio Assessment

Classroom Floor Plan A

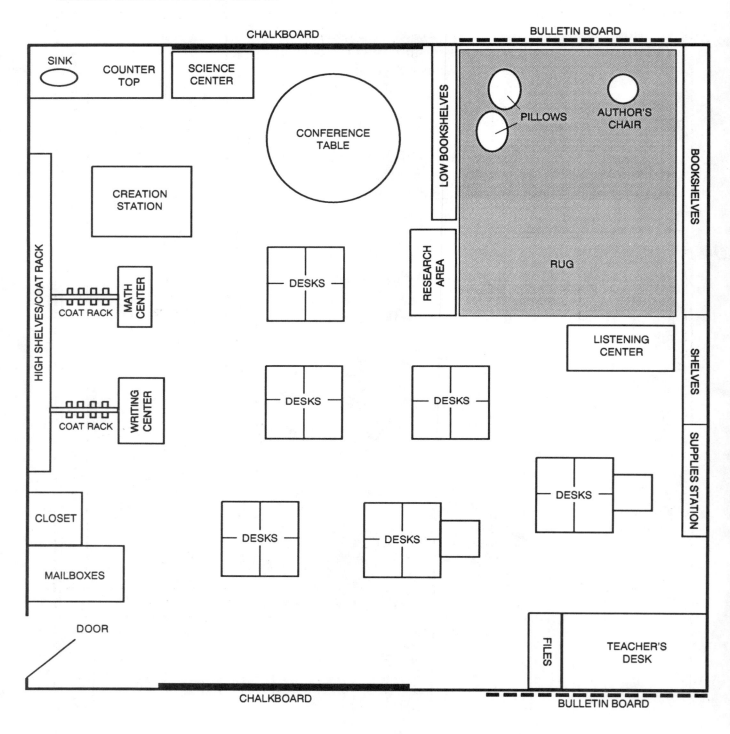

Classroom Floor Plan B

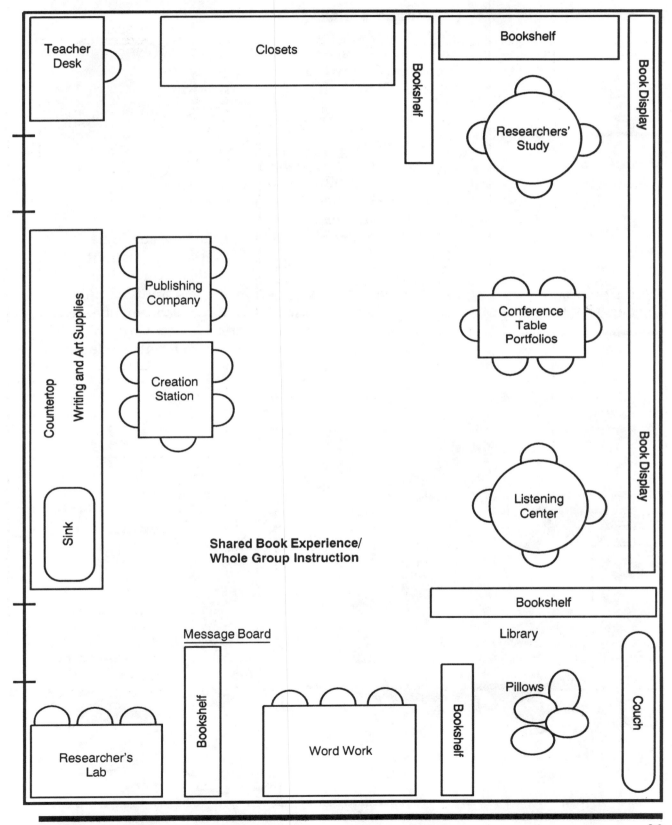

B. Assessment and Evaluation

Assessment and evaluation are an ongoing part of a balanced literacy program. While the teacher facilitates and instructs, she also observes, records, and collects work samples. Students are trusted and given responsibility. During conferences, students learn to collect samples and evaluate their own work. The teacher makes curricular decisions based on what she observes throughout the day. For example, she reads a child's sample from the writing workshop and decides to do a mini-lesson on the use of quotation marks. This integration of assessment, evaluation and instruction is necessary to provide a balanced literacy program for all students.

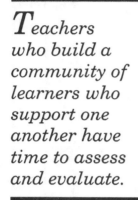

Teachers who build a community of learners who support one another have time to assess and evaluate.

C. Personal Connections and Social Interactions

Personal connections and social interactions are a vital part of a balanced literacy program. Language learning is a very social affair. Language development is encouraged when there are meaningful interactions among children, and between the children and the teacher in a language-rich environment.

A. Rich Literacy Experience

B. Assessment Evaluation

C. Personal Connections Social Interactions

Children need opportunities to respond to books in personally meaningful ways. For example, a child responds to the book *Alexander, and the Terrible, Horrible, No Good, Very Bad Day* by writing a new story about her own terrible day. Then she sits in the author's chair and shares the story by reading it aloud, inviting the audience to react.

Experiences that Promote Literacy Development

As teachers move away from a single approach to teaching, they provide a broader program which integrates the processes of language. The following ten experiences work together to promote children's literacy development. These experiences provide necessary instruction and a learning environment that meets the needs of all students. Children benefit in different ways and to different degrees from these experiences.

✎ Reading Aloud

Reading to children models the actions of a good reader, and the rewards that come from a book. Read aloud to familiarize students with book language. Books from all genres become models for children's writing.

✎ Shared Reading

Reading with a group of children provides a non-threatening experience. The teacher uses an enlarged text (big books, songs, poems) and novels to replicate the bedtime story experience with its intimacy and enjoyment of books. This is a chance to teach the strategies and skills children need for independent reading.

✎ Guided Reading

A teacher works with a small group of children, coaching them through a specially selected text. This text needs to be supportive in order to ensure a successful reading experience, yet challenging enough to help develop reading strategies.

✎ Independent Reading

Self-monitored reading gives children opportunities to gain confidence in their ability to read successfully. Children need practice selecting books that match their interests and abilities.

✎ Responses

These are a record of a child's reaction to reading. Responses reflect a child's thinking and feelings about a text.

what I read little willy was going to enter a race a sled race the winner what win five hundert dollars gest enf money to pay the taxs.

what I think little willy is going to win the five hunderd dollars.

✎ Writing

Children use their background knowledge and experience to write for their own purposes. They experience the writing process from prewriting to publication.

Once upon a time

✎ Modeled Writing

Here a teacher writes in front of the children, demonstrating her own strategies as a proficient writer. She talks aloud as she writes so children learn the writing process through modeling.

✎ Language Experience

Writing down a child's language (dictation) helps make the connection between the spoken and written forms of language. The teacher does the writing and the child does the talking.

The Development of Writing, Spelling and Reading

In the following section we look at how language develops. Increasing our knowledge about children's language development directly affects the observations and evaluations we make.

Children's language learning is unique in that it progresses in specific stages along a developmental continuum. As we observe children we begin to see specific behaviors as indicators or markers of growth. Not all children move through the language developmental stages sequentially, some skip stages, and some children show development at more than one stage at a time. For example, in the spelling sample below, the child moves within the semiphonetic and phonetic spelling stages.

Here we see the child use initial consonants to spell loi (like) and du (drink)—indicating he is in the semiphonetic spelling stage. Yet he also writes stron (strong) with a complete blend and correct vowel, indicating the phonetic stage.

DEC 0 1 1989

I LOiTO iD UXXX
MiLC
BCS MiLC MIU
StRON
N MiLC
MiLC

I like to eat milk because milk makes you strong and milk milk.

I like to drink milk because
milk makes you strong
and milk milk

In language development, errors children make are valuable sources of information about their growth. We can locate where they are and where they have been and then provide classroom experiences to encourage their development.

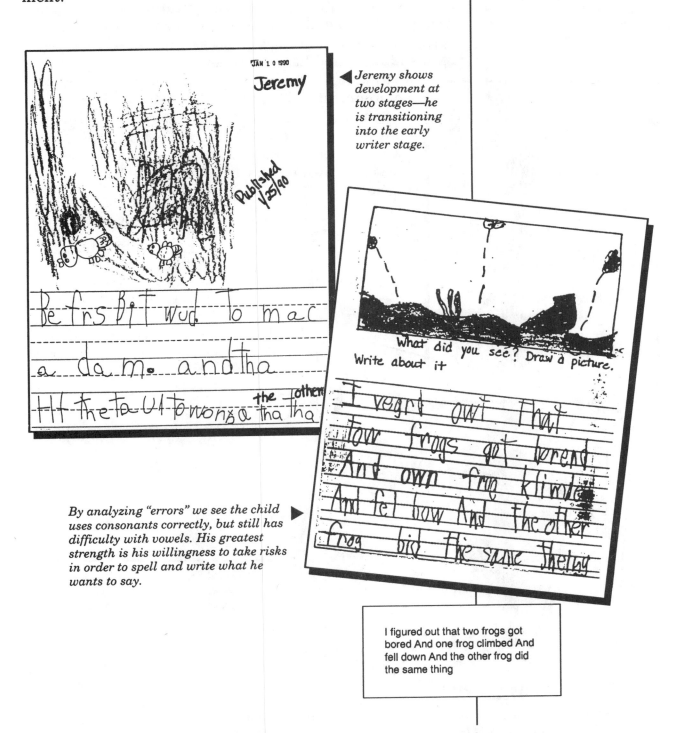

Jeremy shows development at two stages—he is transitioning into the early writer stage.

By analyzing "errors" we see the child uses consonants correctly, but still has difficulty with vowels. His greatest strength is his willingness to take risks in order to spell and write what he wants to say.

I figured out that two frogs got bored And one frog climbed And fell down And the other frog did the same thing

The Three Stages of Writing Development

1. The Emergent Writer

An emergent writer is one who is imitating writing. This writer is often a child who has been read to and has had opportunities to interact with books. He has seen people read and write and has experimented with paper and writing tools. He is beginning to notice print in his environment, such as the McDonald's or Burger King signs, and the print on cereal boxes. The emergent writer may scribble, draw a picture, write his own name or write a few letters in his name. He can reread his own writing or read picture books by memory.

This writer uses letters, numbers, symbols and scribbles to write a story. The writer has established left-to-right directional movement but no sound / symbol relationship.

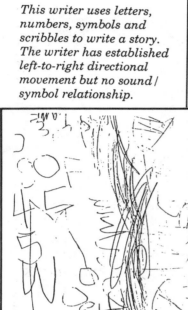

The child has established left-to-right direction, and uses sound / symbol relationships. There are spaces between the words. This writer is transitioning into the early writer stage.

Andy uses beginning, medial and final consonants but is not writing sentences yet. Andy should be encouraged to take risks in his writing.

The Emergent Writer	**Classroom Experiences to Emphasize**

The Emergent Writer

- Draws a picture to write a story

- Engages in scribble writing or symbol writing

- Understands that writing is talk written down

- Uses left-to-right directional movement

- Tells a story or reads "writing" to others

- Uses approximations in writing

- Uses initial consonants

- Uses spaces between words

- Takes risks in writing

- Uses frames for writing

- Self-selects writing topics

Classroom Experiences to Emphasize

✓ Teacher reads aloud from all genres for writing models

✓ Student self-selects topics

✓ Student has opportunities to write and share writing daily

✓ Teacher models writing

✓ Teacher uses language experience to write down a child's talk

2. The Early Writer

An early writer understands that speech can be written down. This writer is beginning to realize that conventions control writing and that writing can be reread. The child does quite a bit of erasing as she struggles with conventions, letter formation and spelling. She rereads to regain understanding lost during these spelling and handwriting struggles.

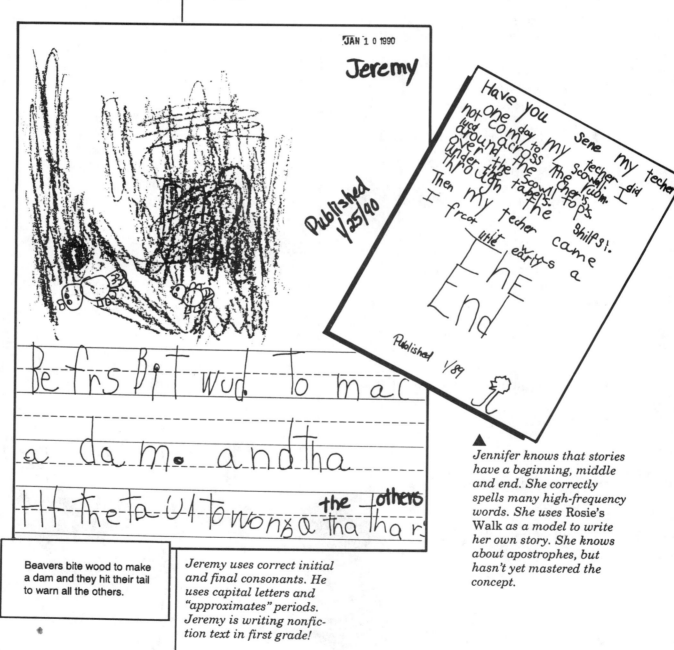

Beavers bite wood to make a dam and they hit their tail to warn all the others.

Jeremy uses correct initial and final consonants. He uses capital letters and "approximates" periods. Jeremy is writing nonfiction text in first grade!

Jennifer knows that stories have a beginning, middle and end. She correctly spells many high-frequency words. She uses Rosie's Walk as a model to write her own story. She knows about apostrophes, but hasn't yet mastered the concept.

The Early Writer	*Classroom Experiences to Emphasize*
•❖ Uses approximate spelling but is moving toward correct spelling	✓ Teacher reads aloud from all genres for writing models
•❖ Uses initial and final consonant sounds correctly	✓ Student self-selects topics
•❖ Places vowels correctly within a word, but not necessarily the *correct* vowel	✓ Student uses the writing process daily—primarily prewriting and rough drafts. The teacher assists with rewriting and the child illustrates for publication
•❖ Spells many high-frequency words	✓ Student has opportunities to share writing
•❖ Uses book models and patterns to help with writing	✓ Teacher models writing
•❖ Chooses own title for a story	✓ Student conferences with teacher and peers
•❖ Includes a simple beginning, middle, and end in a story	✓ Student needs many models and demonstrations of how print works—shared reading, guided reading and writing
•❖ Begins using dialogue	✓ Teacher gives positive responses to the student's approximations
•❖ Uses editing skills—capitals and periods, circles misspelled words	
•❖ Begins to consult classroom resources in order to correct approximations	
•❖ Establishes a personal style	

3. The Fluent Writer

The fluent writer has gradually gained control over writing conventions and letter formations and is therefore writing with ease. He realizes the many purposes for writing. He refines his writing to say what he means and cares about quality. The fluent writer initiates rewriting and revision. He takes more time to complete his text and is conscious of how he "goes about writing." He talks about his and others' writing. He sees that writing involves more than conventions and recognizes the need for developing a theme with detail.

This is Diana's own pre-writing style. She is a fluent writer who knows how to choose a topic and organize her story.

①

Zebra ~~are this~~
Joined the air force. Got arrested ~~Got~~ ran over by a truck He couldn't unzip his pajamis.
He went to a costume party.

-beginning The zebra exscaped from the zoo.

Middle The zebra hides in a cave.

-Ending- The zebra ends up. ~~trying the~~
n a jail sell.

Here is Diana's beginning rough draft. She correctly uses punctuation and other grammar conventions. She needs help in forming paragraphs.

②
escaped
How the Zebra ~~Got Its~~ Stripes
One day a zebra (escaped) from the zoo. Everybody was after him. The police, Army, the Air Force, and even the little boy who lived down the lane. He ran into a horse stable and no one could find him. When the coast was clear he came out of a horse stall and said, "Thank goodness I look like a big fat pony!!!" Then he saw a cave and hid in it and said, "Good thing cave is near the stable. Now I won't go hungry." Then he heard a roaring sound. He looked behind him and saw a big black bear. He ran out of the cave and in the stable. "At least I'll be safe here." Then the bear burst through the door. The zebra got out of the stall and ran away. Finally he got away from the bear. Then zebra was walking down the street. Then people ran out of a bank and gave the

Vanessa finds it easy to tell about a story she wrote. It is clear that she finds writing to be a "joy!"

May 14, 1992

Memories are the best, and keeping them on a sigle piece of paper can help preserve those wonderful memories.

This story taught me that if you want to have something to remember, and be proud of you can just yoop up anything that comes to your mind, you have to think and work at it.

"Horses of The Broken Horn" showed me that if I want to do it I must moooo It!

This story was a joy for me to write because I loved to write and I also love to ride Horses so I combined them into 1, my most loved piece.

Vanessa ♡

The Fluent Writer	*Classroom Experiences to Emphasize*
●◆ Develops a beginning, middle, and end to a story	✓ Teacher reads aloud from all genres for writing models—topic development, story structure, language usage
●◆ Reads for more information to include in writing	✓ Student self-selects topics
●◆ Demonstrates knowledge about the subject	✓ Student uses the writing process daily—the entire writing process: revisions, rewriting, and publishing by the student
●◆ Develops a theme or topic with details	
●◆ Writes in a variety of genres	✓ Teacher models writing—how to revise and work on a text in order to fulfill the writer's intentions and meet the readers' needs
●◆ Uses word endings correctly	
●◆ Makes verb tenses agree throughout writing	✓ Student has opportunities to share writing
●◆ Writes in paragraphs	✓ Student conferences with peers
●◆ Uses correct punctuation—exclamation point, question mark, comma, quotation marks	✓ Student conferences with teacher—conversations, strategies, final editing
●◆ Self-initiates editing	
●◆ Self-initiates revision	
●◆ Shows concern for quality	

Spelling as a Part of Writing

In *Spel . . . Is A Four Letter Word*, author Richard Gentry shares the current research on spelling development. This research indicates there is no relationship between I.Q. and spelling ability, and that spelling is a complex cognitive process rather than a simple memorization task. Visual memory, crucial to spelling, is not an acquired skill but one you are born with. **Most importantly, research shows that spelling is best learned when taught within the context of writing.**

Instruction, assessment and evaluation of spelling should take place within the meaningful context of writing.

Gentry, as well as other experts, has identified broad developmental stages in learning to spell. Children begin with gross approximations of correct spelling, and work towards self-correction. Children develop through their own self-regulation and motivation. Teachers give input and model how to spell words. Instruction should match the developmental level of the child.

The following pages describe the stages of spelling development and how a child moves toward conventional spelling along a developmental continuum.

Spelling is a complex cognitive process rather than a simple memorization task.

Stages of Spelling Development

1. Precommunicative Stage

At this stage the child scribbles or uses symbols, such as numbers and shapes, in order to write. Drawings almost always accompany writing. There is often no left to right progression, just random placement of the symbols, shapes and scribbles.

Paul strings together the letters of his name. He is not yet aware of sound / symbol relationships. He writes using left-to-right progression.

Matthew says this is a list of his aunts, uncles and cousins. His scribbles tell the story.

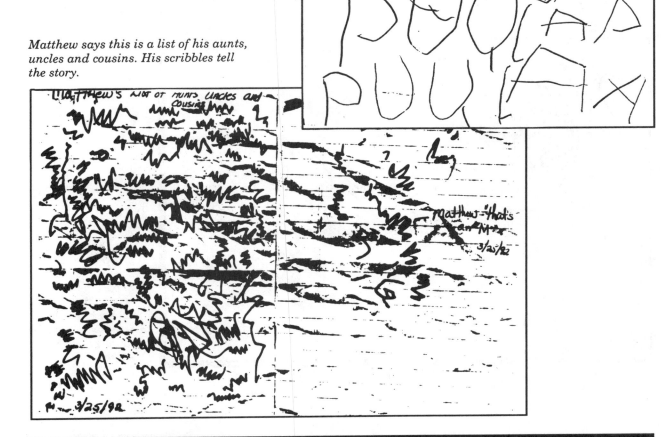

2. Semiphonetic Stage

At this stage the child begins her first attempts at sound-symbol correspondence. For example, she writes *I L P* for "I like pizza." She may also string together letters of her name in order to write a message. There may be some spaces between words.

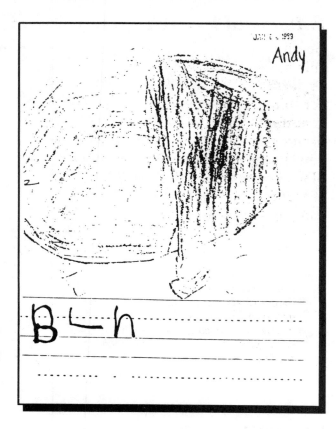

Andy understands the sound / symbol relationship as he writes BLN for "balloon." He will probably soon be adding vowels to his words.

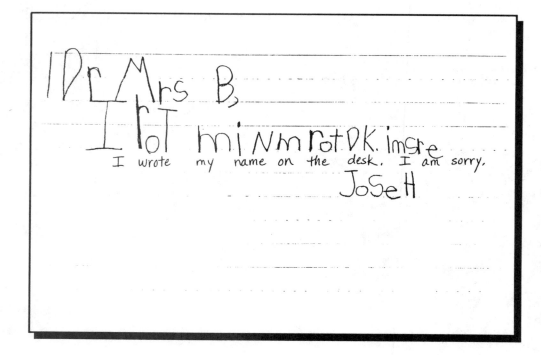

Jose has a good grasp of initial consonants. He knows there are medial and final consonants. He is transitioning to the phonetic stage.

3. Phonetic Stage

Spelling is not conventional at this stage, but it is more easily understood. Initial and final consonants are in place. The child gradually adds interior consonants and vowels. Often the vowels are not correct, but are placed correctly in the word. Left to right progression and word spacing are clearly evident.

▶

Pamela correctly writes most consonants (beginning, medial, final). Her vowels are in the correct place, but she doesn't always use the correct vowel. Pamela spells phonetically, using the sounds of the letters.

Adam's vowel approximations are appropriate. He is moving towards the transitional stage.

▼

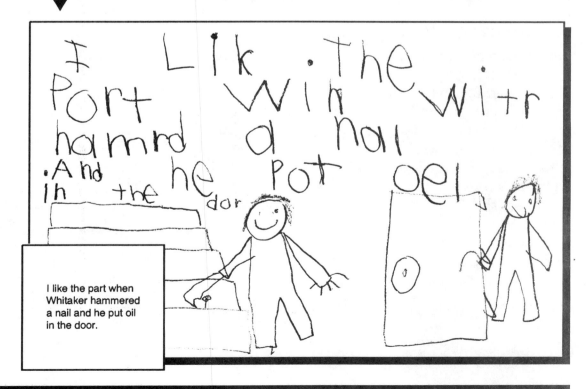

I like the part when Whitaker hammered a nail and he put oil in the door.

4. Transitional Stage

At this stage the child's writing has more correctly spelled words. Vowel letter approximations are more accurate and word endings are spelled conventionally. Often all the letters necessary to spell the word are there but they may be in the wrong order. For example, *becuase* for "because."

Dat uses English as a second language, so he writes like he speaks. He spells most words correctly and approximates some vowels. He does not allow his spelling to hinder communication—he writes what he wants to say.

> Ben Franklin is a printer s intist he made swimming paddle he descover ilick trsody is lightning and he was born 1706.

> In the 1840, people travle with wagin weels becuase they didn't have no car in the 1840.

> Dat   Jan 24 1992
> In the 1840 kids don't play with Nintendo and Gameboy they just go out to a tree and made a swing By it are just play with a doll are jump on there bed.

> They live in a log cabin not in a house are a apatmat.

5. Correct Spelling

Knowledge of the spelling system is firmly established at this stage. The child recognizes when the word doesn't look right and experiments with alternatives. A large number of words are spelled automatically. When unsure of a word, the child uses dictionaries and other resources to correct the spelling.

Amanda has a solid under-standing of spelling. She tells the reader that she spells "uniquely" at times, so we realize she knows her words don't always look right.

> May 14, 1992
>
> Dear Reader,
>   I chose this supier piece of writing because it's about me I me, the great Amanda Campa I I also really think I have inhanced my writing ability, even though the spelling is a little "unique." ☺
>   I was just sittin around the house fliping through all the cable chanles when I got my idea to just write about my self! I think I did a pretty good job at it, I received an "A" on my biography!
>   I hope you enjoy reading about me, Amanda Campa, and see the person deep down in side me. So good luck, and enjoy!
>
>   —Amanda
>   author of
>   "Wierd or Unique"

The Reading Process

Reading is an active thinking process in which the reader learns to use various strategies in order to gain meaning from print. Some strategies include:

- looking at picture clues
- rereading when the text doesn't make sense
- substituting another word for an unknown word
- learning to predict

Children will direct their own learning and seek improvement if they are allowed to approximate. Short, in *Bridges to Literacy* (1991), describes the benefits of teaching reading strategies rather than reading skills:

> *Instead of the teacher working to drill several skills to "mastery," readers experience the use of a wide range of strategies from which they can choose when they encounter difficulty during reading. These strategies differ radically from most "scope and sequence" lists of skills, which contain specific items to memorize, such as certain letter sounds or vowel rules. Teaching for strategies focuses at a more general level on the processes that use these specific items. Students still often learn many of these more specific skills, but they do so as they actually read and write rather than through direct, isolated instruction.*

On the following pages we see how the reading process works and how the cueing systems work together.

When children read they draw from the three cueing systems explained below. In order to make sense of print, children need to integrate these cueing systems within the reading process. Running records are an evaluative tool to help identify the cueing systems children use.

Reading Cueing Systems

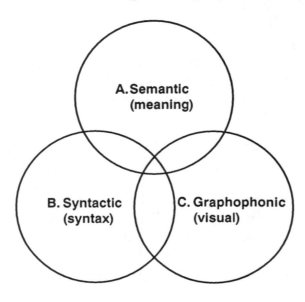

A. Semantic

The semantic (meaning) cueing system helps readers relate their own experiences and background to what they are reading. For example, when reading the sentence, *It was too hot in the classroom, so the teacher turned on the _____,* children predict the last word by drawing upon their background knowledge.

B. Syntactic

The syntactic cueing system helps readers use their knowledge of word order, sentence order, and grammar. For example, in the sentence, *It was too hot in the classroom so the teacher turned on the _____ ,* readers will choose a noun for the last word, rather than a verb or adjective, because of their expertise and understanding of how language works.

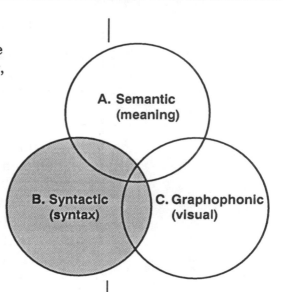

C. Graphophonic

The graphophonic (visual) cueing system helps readers with the letters and sounds of the language. For example, the reader sees the text, *My dog Sam takes a bath,* but reads, "My dog Sam takes a shower." The reader may then hesitate, take a closer look at letter detail, and self-correct. This cueing system is the most difficult for early readers to use.

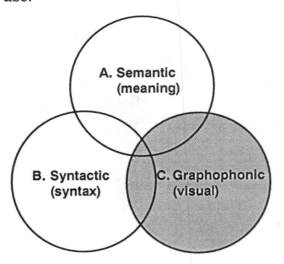

The Three Stages of Reading Development

1. The Emergent Reader

The child at this stage exhibits "reading-like" behavior as she reads stories over and over. This is actually an approximation and retelling of the text as the reader relies on her memory and her experience with the story in order to read it. The child asks others to read her favorite stories and is very aware when a reader leaves out part of the text. She notices environmental print and reads familiar signs. The emergent reader is developing an appetite and curiosity for understanding what print is all about. She is beginning to see that print, as well as illustrations, carries a meaningful message.

Choosing Books

The emergent reader needs text that is highly predictable. The story should be told in the illustrations. The text should match the oral language of the reader.

Book titles include:

Have You Seen My Cat?
Brian Wildsmith

One Hunter
Pat Hutchins

Rain
Robert Kaplan

The Chick and the Duckling
Mirra Ginsburg

Emergent Reader Inventory

Key
N-Not observed
B-Beginning
S-Secure

Name: Sarah   Date of Birth: _____

EMERGENT READER BEHAVIORS	K 9/92			Anecdotal Notes
Uses reading-like behavior to approximate book language	S			9/24 Sarah pretend reads "Brown Bear." Tries to point to the words. Doesn't have one-to-one matching.
Notices/reads environmental print	S			
Recognizes some high frequency words	N			10/5 Brought in labels from K-Mart and McDonalds. to show what she could read.
Retells favorite stories	S			
Memorizes rhymes and poems	S			
Knows what a letter is	B			
Knows what a word is	B			
Knows some letters and sounds	N			
Knows that letter symbols form words	N			
Knows that text goes L to R	S			
Knows where to start reading the text	S			
Is establishing 1-to-1 correspondence	B			
Enjoys writing	B			
Enjoys shared experiences with books	S			

The Emergent Reader	*Classroom Experiences to Emphasize*
●◆ Uses reading-like behavior to approximate book language	✓ Teacher emphasizes language experience—writing down a child's talk
●◆ Notices and reads environmental print	✓ Student and teacher participate in shared reading
●◆ Retells favorite stories, memorizes rhymes and poems	✓ Teacher reads aloud from all genres
●◆ Is starting to enjoy reading	✓ Student rereads familiar text
●◆ Understands the difference between letters and words	✓ Teacher begins guided reading using very predictable natural language texts
●◆ Recognizes some high-frequency words	
●◆ Knows quite a few letters	
●◆ Understands that writers use letter symbols to form words	
●◆ Knows that text goes from left to right	
●◆ Knows where to start reading the text	
●◆ Is establishing one-to-one correspondence	

2. The Early Reader

The early reader is moving from "reading-like" behavior to word-by-word reading. He may point with his finger as he reads. He no longer memorizes favorite stories, but tries to match a printed word with a spoken word, and he expects the stories to make sense. This reader chooses to read independently, and is very excited about his ability to do so. The early reader begins to develop a variety of reading strategies—such as rereading when the text doesn't make sense, applying his experience of oral language to the text, and confirming his predictions by checking visual cues. This reader reads and rereads many books with a high level of accuracy.

Choosing Books

The early reader needs text that is somewhat predictable or repetitive. The story is told in the words, with some picture support. The text is more like written rather than spoken language.

Book titles include:

Rosie's Walk
Pat Hutchins

Mouse Soup
Arnold Lobel

Frog and Toad
Arnold Lobel

Early Reader Inventory

Key
N-Not observed
B-Beginning
S-Secure

Name: _Carlos_   Date of Birth: _____

EARLY READER BEHAVIORS	Grade/Date 12/91	5/92		Anecdotal Notes
Has established 1 to-1 correspondence	S			12/2 Points to the text, word by word, as he reads "Whose Mouse Are You?"
Chooses to read independently	N			
Expects to get meaning from print	S			12/30 Came to an unknown word, stopped, looked at the picture & reread — correcting the error.
Takes risks with unfamiliar text	B			
Reads word-by-word with finger or voice	S			
Begins to integrate strategies and cross-check cueing systems:				
⇨ Rereads when it doesn't make sense	S			
⇨ Self-corrects errors	B			
⇨ Relies more on visual cues than pictures	B			
Recognizes high-frequency words out of context	S			
Spells some high-frequency words correctly	S			
Enjoys writing	S			
Uses resources to help spell words	B			
Enjoys shared reading experiences	S			

Creative Teaching Press

The Early Reader	*Classroom Experiences to Emphasize*
●◆ Has established one-to-one correspondence	✓ Student and teacher participate in shared reading
●◆ Chooses to read independently	✓ Teacher models tracking of print, emphasizing how the text carries the story
●◆ Expects to get meaning and enjoyment from print	✓ Teacher reads aloud from all genres
●◆ Takes risks in reading unfamiliar text	✓ Teacher uses guided reading with graduated natural language texts
●◆ Reads word by word and may point with finger	✓ Student reads independently from texts which can be read with a high degree of accuracy
●◆ Repeats words or rereads text when it doesn't make sense	✓ Student reads independently and is encouraged to take risks
●◆ Self-corrects when there is realization of an error	
●◆ Builds a vocabulary of sight words	
●◆ Begins to integrate strategies and cross-checks cueing systems	
●◆ Relies more on visual cues than picture cues	
●◆ Enjoys writing and uses resources in the classroom to help with spelling	
●◆ Begins to identify misspelled words in his writing	
●◆ Spells some high-frequency words correctly	

3. The Fluent Reader

The fluent reader is very interested in different kinds of text. She moves into silent reading, and works on her strategies until she has control over the reading process. Because of this, she reads more difficult material and greater quantities of text. At this stage a reader, in order to work out difficult text, may revert to word-by-word reading, characteristic of the early reader. This type of flexibility is a sign of developed reading behavior. The book choices this reader makes reflect her level of experience with texts. A less-experienced fluent reader chooses short books with illustrations, comic books, and magazines. An experienced fluent reader chooses books which interest her and is able to use a variety of sources to research a topic.

Choosing Books

The fluent reader can handle a broad range of text. Less experienced readers need short chapters and more illustrations. More experienced readers move into text with difficult vocabulary and abstract ideas.

Book titles include:

Nate the Great
Marjorie Sharmat

Kids of Polk Street School
Patricia Giff

Stone Fox
John Gardiner

Hatchet
Gary Paulsen

Fluent Reader Inventory

Key
N-Not observed
B-Beginning
S-Secure

Name: Desiree   Date of Birth: _____

FLUENT READER BEHAVIORS	3rd 9/91	3rd 4/92	4th 10/92	Anecdotal Notes
Integrates strategies automatically and cross-checks cueing systems	S			3/5 Hooked on Beverly Cleary books. She says, "I'm a lot like Ramona you know. We should be sisters."
Uses strategies flexibly for familiar and unfamiliar text	B	S		
Has a large sight word vocabulary	S			4/30 Showing an interest in nonfiction books. Says she likes to research interesting facts.
Moves from reading aloud to reading silently	S			
Chooses appropriate books for own purposes	S	B		
Reads a series of books written by a favorite author	B	S		
Reads short chapter books with the support of pictures	S			
Reads chapter books for longer periods of time	B	S		
Responses show reflection from different points of view	S			
Reads books to pursue particular interests	N		B	
Reads informational books but still needs support with expository text	B			
Realizes that different texts demand different strategies	B		S	
Is capable of reading different kinds of text across the curriculum	B			
Reads a variety of sources to independently research a topic	B			
Has developed a personal taste in fiction and/or nonfiction books	B	S		

Portfolio Assessment   Creative Teaching Press

The Fluent Reader	*Classroom Experiences to Emphasize*
●◆ Integrates strategies automatically and cross-checks cueing systems	✓ Student and teacher participate in shared reading (including novels)
●◆ Has a large sight word vocabulary	✓ Teacher reads aloud from all genres
●◆ Reads silently	✓ Teacher uses guided reading with nonfiction and fiction texts
●◆ Uses strategies flexibly to read familiar and unfamiliar texts	✓ Student is reading to learn
●◆ Chooses appropriate books for his/her purpose	✓ Student participates in literature circles
●◆ Reads short chapter books with the support of pictures; magazines, and comic books	✓ Student engages in buddy and individualized reading
●◆ Reads chapter books for gradually longer periods	✓ Student reads independently from books he can read with a high degree of accuracy
●◆ Reads informational books, but still needs support with expository text	
●◆ Reads from a variety of sources to independently research a topic	
●◆ Reads books to pursue a particular interest	
●◆ Has developed a personal taste for certain types of books	

Notes

Part IV

Resources

9. *Forms and Checklists*

WARNING:

**CHECKLISTS CAN BE HAZARDOUS
TO YOUR HEALTH
IF YOU TRY TO IMPLEMENT THEM
ALL AT ONCE!**

It is recommended that you use checklists for a variety of purposes including:

✓ Identifying and diagnosing instructional needs
✓ Planning goals and instruction for your classroom
✓ Increasing your understanding of language development
✓ Empowering your observations and anecdotal records
✓ Adapting and developing your own lists

Emergent Reader Inventory

Name: _____ Date of Birth: _____

EMERGENT READER BEHAVIORS	Grade/Date				Anecdotal Notes
Uses reading-like behavior to approximate book language					
Notices/reads environmental print					
Recognizes some high-frequency words					
Retells favorite stories					
Memorizes rhymes and poems					
Knows what a letter is					
Knows what a word is					
Knows some letters and sounds					
Knows that letter symbols form words					
Knows that text goes L to R					
Knows where to start reading the text					
Is establishing 1-to-1 correspondence					
Enjoys writing					
Enjoys shared experiences with books					

Early Reader Inventory

Name: _____ Date of Birth: _____

	Grade/Date				Anecdotal Notes
EARLY READER BEHAVIORS					
Has established 1-to-1 correspondence					
Chooses to read independently					
Expects to get meaning from print					
Takes risks with unfamiliar text					
Reads word-by-word with finger or voice					
Begins to integrate strategies and cross-check cueing systems: ∽ Rereads when it doesn't make sense ∽ Self-corrects errors ∽ Relies more on visual cues than pictures					
Recognizes high-frequency words out of context					
Spells some high-frequency words correctly					
Enjoys writing					
Uses resources to help spell words					
Enjoys shared reading experiences					

Portfolio Assessment
Creative Teaching Press

Fluent Reader Inventory

Name: _____ Date of Birth: _____

FLUENT READER BEHAVIORS	Grade/Date				Anecdotal Notes
Integrates strategies automatically and cross-checks cueing systems					
Uses strategies flexibly for familiar and unfamiliar text					
Has a large sight word vocabulary					
Moves from reading aloud to reading silently					
Chooses appropriate books for own purposes					
Reads a series of books written by a favorite author					
Reads short chapter books with the support of pictures					
Reads chapter books for longer periods of time					
Responses show reflection from different points of view					
Reads books to pursue particular interests					
Reads informational books but still needs support with expository text					
Realizes that different texts demand different strategies					
Is capable of reading different kinds of text across the curriculum					
Reads a variety of sources to independently research a topic					
Has developed a personal taste for fiction and/or nonfiction books					

STUDENT READING SURVEY

Name:_____ Date: _____

1. How did you learn to read?

2. What is your favorite kind of book?

3. Who is your favorite author?

4. What books have you reread? Why do you reread them?

5. How many books do you think you've read in the last year?

6. Does your family own books at home? Do you own books and keep them in your room?

7. How often do you visit the library?

8. Do you like it when your teacher reads to you?

9. Given a choice, would you rather watch TV or read?

10. What do you think a good reader is?

11. Do all people need to learn to read?

12. Is it important to learn to read? Why or why not?

Portfolio Assessment Creative Teaching Press

MY READING LOG

Name _____

Date	Title/Author	Genre

MY HOME READING LOG

Name _____

Date	Title/Author	

Portfolio Assessment

Creative Teaching Press

My Published Books

by_____

Date	Title	Genre

Written Language Inventory

Emergent and Early Writer (Side 1)

Name: _____ Date of Birth: _____

THE WRITING PROCESS	Grade/Date				Anecdotal Notes
Uses a picture to write					
Uses scribbles or symbols					
Random use of letters, symbols					
L to R directional movement					
Understands that writing symbolizes talk written down					
Chooses own topic					
Reads writing to others					
Takes risks in writing					
Personal voice heard in writing					
Innovates on language patterns					
Uses simple beginning, middle, end					
Writes title for story					
Matches illustrations to text					
Attempts to write in different modes: story or tale, letter, diary					
Uses beginning editing skills: capitals and periods circles words misspelled					

Portfolio Assessment

Creative Teaching Press

Written Language Inventory

Emergent and Early Writer (Side 2)

Name _____

	Grade/Date				Anecdotal Notes
PUNCTUATION/CAPITALIZATION					
Uses periods					
Is aware of question marks, exclamation points, commas, quotation marks					
Uses capitals at the beginning of sentences					
Uses capitals for most proper nouns					
SPELLING					
Random use of symbols, scribbles, letters					
Uses initial consonants					
L to R progression in words					
Spaces between words					
Takes risks in spelling					
Uses initial, final consonants					
Conventional spelling of some words					
Uses incorrect vowel but in correct place					
Conventional spelling of word endings					
Vowel approximations are more accurate					
Recognizes misspellings					
Uses classroom resources to check spelling					
GRAMMAR					
Uses complete sentences					
Uses compound sentences linked by "and"					

Written Language Inventory

Fluent Writer (Side 1)

Name: _____ Date of Birth: _____

	Grade/Date				Anecdotal Notes
WRITING PROCESS					
Self-selects topics					
Fully developed beginning, middle, end					
Reads for information to include in writing					
Develops writing topic with details					
Summarizes information in own words					
Writes within all domains: narrative/descriptive informative/expository					
Understands his/her own writing process					
Writing is meaningful and enjoyable					
Prewriting or rehearsal strategies					
Takes notes, makes lists Collaborates, talks Uses clustering, mapping Uses outlines					
Rough draft					
Writes for a purpose and audience Willing to take risks Uses a word processor					
Revising					
Initiates revision Willingly shares writing Gives and receives advice					
Editing					
Self-initiates editing Uses editing conventions					
Publishing					
Sees self as an author Shares finished piece					

Portfolio Assessment

Creative Teaching Press

Written Language Inventory

Fluent Writer (Side 2)

Name: _____

	Grade/Date				Anecdotal Notes
PUNCTUATION/CAPITALIZATION					
Uses ending punctuation (. ? !)					
Uses commas					
Uses quotation marks					
Uses appropriate capitalization					
GRAMMAR					
Uses verb tense agreement throughout writing					
Uses subject/predicate agreement					
Uses paragraphs					
Varies sentence beginnings					
Uses figures of speech					
SPELLING					
Marks approximations for checking later					
Spells a large collection of words automatically					
Uses resources to check spelling					

Writing Survey

Name: _____ Date: _____

1. Do you consider yourself an author? Why? Why not?

2. Why do you think people write?

3. Do you think most people like to write?

4. Do your parents write? If so, what do they usually write?

5. Who is your favorite author? Why?

6. Are there any books by a particular author that have changed the way you write?

7. How do you decide what you're going to write about?

8. What are your favorite topics to write about?

9. When and where do you like to write?

10. What helps you to write?

Portfolio Assessment

Creative Teaching Press

My Writing

Name: _____ Date: _____

Circle your answer:

1. I like to write.   YES   NO   MAYBE

2. I like to publish my writing.   YES   NO   MAYBE

3. I am a real author.   YES   NO   MAYBE

4. I like to sit on the author's
   chair and share my writing.   YES   NO   MAYBE

5. My family likes to read my books.   YES   NO   MAYBE

6. Kids in our class help me write.   YES   NO   MAYBE

7. The hardest thing about writing is . . .

_____

_____

═══════════ Here's a sample of my writing ═══════════

_____'s Ideas for Writing

_____

_____

_____

_____

_____

_____

_____

_____

_____

_____

_____

_____

_____

Portfolio Assessment

Name_____

In My Writing . . .

I can _____

_____

_____

_____

_____

_____

_____

I am working on _____

_____

_____

_____

_____

_____

_____

My Reading

Name:_____ Date:_____

Circle your answer:

1. I like to read.   YES   NO   MAYBE

2. I like my parents and teacher to read to me.   YES   NO   MAYBE

3. I have a favorite author.   YES   NO   MAYBE

4. I go to the library.   YES   NO   MAYBE

5. I think reading is important.   YES   NO   MAYBE

6. I have books of my own at home.   YES   NO   MAYBE

7. I like to tell others about the books I read.   YES   NO   MAYBE

Draw a picture about your favorite book.

Conference Record

Name_____ Date _____

Reading/ Writing	Observations	Instructional Need/Goal

Student Portfolio Summary

School Year _____ Student's Name _____

Date/Grade	Summary

Portfolio Assessment Creative Teaching Press

PARENT SURVEY

Family name _____ School Year_____

Child's name_____Date of Birth _____

Name of brothers/sisters _____

_____

What languages are spoken at home? _____

Is there someone at home who can help your child with English ? _____

_____

In what way can you help your child at home with reading and homework? _____

_____

Is your child supposed to wear glasses? Has he/she had a vision test outside school?

_____

Does your child have any physical concerns or special needs that the school should be aware of?

_____

Anecdotal notes of discussions at parent conference   **Date:**

FOR THE PORTFOLIO

Name: _____ Date: _____

✎ ✎ ✎ **Student Comments:**

I chose this work because _____

_____

_____

_____

_____

I think it shows my progress because _____

_____

_____

_____

_____

_____

☙ ☙ ☙ **Parent Comments:**

We or I think that _____'s work shows _____

_____

_____

_____

_____

❧ ❧ ❧ **Teacher Comments:**

I think _____'s work shows_____

_____

_____

_____

_____

Portfolio Assessment Creative Teaching Press

Reflecting on Myself

Name _____ Grade _____

At the beginning, middle and end of the year, rate yourself on the following items.

	(Date)	(Date)	(Date)
I am responsible.			
I do all the work I'm asked to do.			
I ask for help when I need it.			
I check to see that my work is my best.			
I turn my work in on time.			
I am motivated.			
I think learning is important.			
I want to learn.			
I am doing all I am able to do.			
I care about doing my best.			
I am self-confident.			
I believe I can learn.			
I know mistakes are part of learning.			
I learn from my mistakes.			
I can learn even if the work is hard.			
I get along with my classmates.			
I am helpful and friendly.			
I listen to others' ideas.			
I share and take turns.			
I don't use put-downs.			
I talk about problems with my friends.			

How can I improve my work? _____

_____

_____

_____

Kind Compliments

Ask your friends, teacher, parents and classmates to give you positive feedback on your work.

I like the way you:

○

○

○

Signed by

Your work made me think about:

Signed by

I enjoyed:

Your story was interesting because:

Signed by

This is what I have to say about your story:

"

"

Signed by

I enjoyed:

I enjoyed:

Signed by

☆ ☆ ☆
☆
☆

Signed by

I learned this from you:

Signed by

My favorite part is:

Signed by

I enjoyed reading about:

Signed by

Speaking and Listening Record

Name_____

BEHAVIORS TO OBSERVE	Date/Anecdotal Records
Listens . . .	
when the teacher talks	
when the teacher reads	
when another child talks	
during a whole group discussion	
Listens and follows directions	
Listens and responds appropriately to conversations	
Speaks . . .	
to the teacher	
to other children	
in small group discussions	
in large group discussions	
to share personal information	
to formally present information to the class	
Speaking and listening observed in different contexts:	
creation of art/craft projects	
independent science and math experiments	
dramatic play, storytelling, retelling, Reader's Theatre	
social play with peers	
reading and writing in collaborative groups	

10. Bibliography

For those who want to become effective evaluators, there is no replacement for reading professional books and journals.

Assessment and Evaluation

Anthony, Robert J., et al. *Evaluating Literacy: A Perspective for Change.* Heinemann, 1991.

Barrs, Myra, et al. *The Primary Language Record: Handbook for Teachers.* Heinemann, 1988.

Brown, Hazel, and Brian Cambourne. *Read and Retell.* Heinemann, 1989.

Clay, Marie. *The Early Detection of Reading Difficulties.* Heinemann, 1979.

Daly, E. *Monitoring Children's Language Development.* Heinemann, 1991.

Davies, Cooper, Winfield, and Jon, eds. *Portfolio News.* Portfolio Assessment Clearinghouse, Encinitas, CA.

Educational Leadership 49, no. 8 (May, 1992).

Eggleton, Jill. *Whole Language Evaluation: Reading, Writing and Spelling.* The Wright Group, 1990.

Goodman, Kenneth, et al. *The Whole Language Catalog: Supplement on Authentic Assessment.* SRA, 1992.

Goodman, Yetta. "Kid Watching: An Alternative to Testing." *National Elementary Principals* 57, no. 4 (June, 1978): 41–45.

Graves, Donald, and B. Sunstein. *Portfolio Portraits.* Heinemann, 1992.

Literacy Assessment in Practice. Education Department of South Australia. NCTE, 1991.

Paulson, Leon, ed. *Portfolio Assessment Newsletter.* Northwest Evaluation Association, Lake Oswego, OR.

Tierney, Robert J., et al., eds. *Portfolio Assessment in the Reading-Writing Classroom.* Christopher Gordon Publishers, 1991.

Traill, Leanna. *Highlight My Strengths.* Rigby, 1992.

A Balanced Literacy Program

Butler, Andrea. *Staff Development Video Series*. Rigby, 1988. Videotape.

Butler, Andrea, and Jan Turbill. *Towards a Reading-Writing Classroom*. Heinemann, 1987.

Davidson, Avelyn. *Literacy 2000 Teachers' Resource*. Rigby, 1991.

DeFord, Diane, et al., eds. *Bridges to Literacy: Learning From Reading Recovery*. Heinemann, 1991.

Graves, Donald. *Discover Your Own Literacy*. Heinemann, 1990.

Harste, Jerome, et al. *Language Stories and Literacy Lessons*. Heinemann, 1984.

Johnson, Terry, and D. R. Louis. *Bringing It All Together: A Program for Literacy*. Heinemann, 1990.

Mooney, M. *Reading To, With, and By Children*. Richard C. Owen Publishers, 1990.

Routman, Regie. *Invitations: Changing as Teachers and Learners, K–12*. Heinemann, 1991.

Traill, Leanna. *Guided Reading Video: The Wobbly Tooth*. Rigby, 1990. Videotape.

Classroom Management

Brown, H., and V. Mathie. *Inside Whole Language: A Classroom View*. Heinemann, 1991.

Collis, M., and J. Dalton. *Becoming Responsible Learners: Strategies for Positive Classroom Management*. Heinemann, 1990.

Eisele, Beverly. *Managing the Whole Language Classroom*. Creative Teaching Press, 1991.

Gibbs, Jeanne. *Tribes: A Process for Social Development and Cooperative Learning*. Center Source Publications, 1987.

Hohmann, M., et al. *Young Children in Action*. The High/Scope Press, 1979.

Peterson, R. *Life in a Crowded Place: Making a Learning Community*. Heinemann, 1992.

Good Beginnings in Whole Lanugage

Cambourne, Brian. *The Whole Story*. Scholastic, 1988.

Crafton, Linda. *Whole Language: Getting Started . . . Moving Forward*. Richard C. Owen Publishers, 1991.

Manning, Gary and Maryann, eds. *Whole Language: Beliefs and Practices, K–8*. National Education Association, 1989.

Power, B., and R. Hubbard. *The Heinemann Reader: Literacy in Process*. Heinemann, 1991.

Reading

Butler, Andrea. *Exploring Reading Video*. Rigby, 1992. Videotape.

Clay, Marie. *The Early Detection of Reading Difficulties*. 3rd ed. Heinemann, 1985.

Traill, Leanna. *Learning Running Records Video*. Rigby, 1992. Videotape.

————. *Using Running Records Video*. Rigby, 1992. Videotape.

Writing and Spelling

Atwell, Nancy, ed. *Coming to Know: Writing to Learn in the Intermediate Grades*. Heinemann, 1990.

Calkins, Lucy. *The Art of Teaching Writing*. Heinemann, 1986.

Calkins, Lucy, and S. Harwayne. *Living Between the Lines*. Heinemann, 1991.

Cambourne, Brian, and Jan Turbill. *Coping With Chaos*. Heinemann, 1987.

Gentry, J. Richard. *Spel . . . Is a Four-Letter Word*. Heinemann, 1987.

Parry, Jo-Ann, and David Hornsby. *Write On: A Conference Approach to Writing*. Heinemann, 1985.

Principals support teachers by developing professional libraries at the school site, and by giving teachers time to read together.

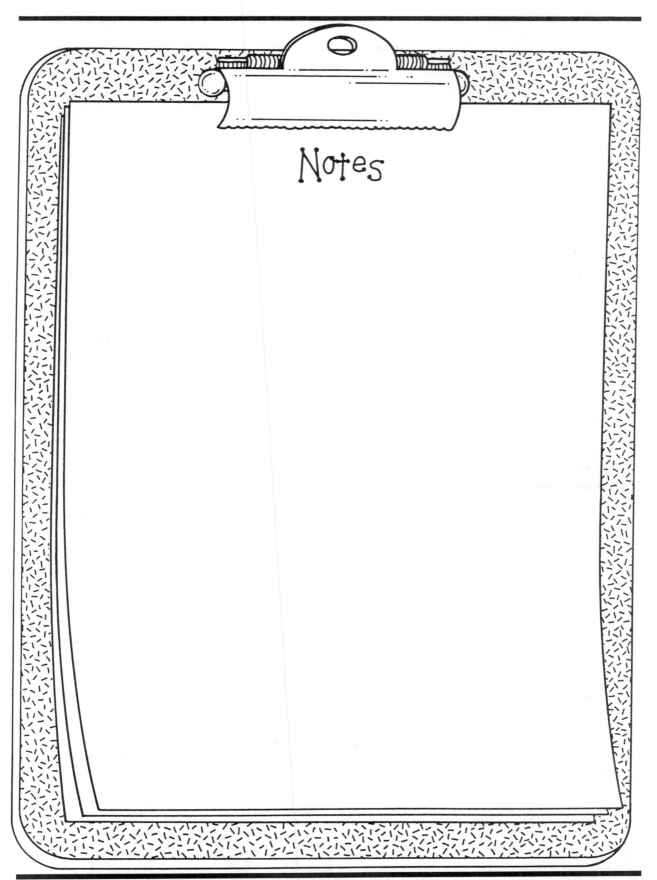

Notes